10657648

Virtual Assistant handbook

ST020042

CORNWALL COLLEGE

the *Virtual Assistant* handbook

Nadine Hill

First Published In Great Britain 2009
by www.BookShaker.com

© Copyright Nadine Hill

All rights reserved. No part of this publication
may be reproduced, stored in or introduced into
a retrieval system, or transmitted, in any form,
or by any means (electronic, mechanical,
photocopying recording or otherwise) without the
prior written permission of the publisher.

This book is sold subject to the condition that it
shall not, by way of trade or otherwise, be lent,
resold, hired out, or otherwise circulated without
the publisher's prior consent in any form of
binding or cover other than that in which it is
published and without a similar condition
including this condition being imposed on the
subsequent purchaser.

Typeset in Trebuchet

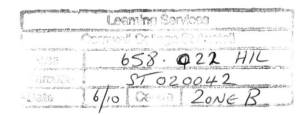

Learning Services

658 . 022 HIL
ST 020042
6/10   2ONE B

*For each and every one of
my valued clients, thank you.*

Contents

Acknowledgements

I've always wondered what I'd say in an 'Oscar acceptance speech' – this is my version of it!

I want to start off by thanking my super support team! My mum, Celia Johnson and my mother-in-law Val Hill. They help me week in, week out with childcare and without their help and loving support, it would have been impossible to find the time to write this book! Your help means more to me than you could ever imagine ladies, thank you.

Thank you to Gillie and the team at Telebizz for their support, friendship and encouragement – we work really well together.

Thank you POW girls, CCC girls and the MYM team. Your continued support, friendship and belief in me means such a lot.

Thanks Dad for always being there. Thank you Debbie Jenkins and Joe Gregory from *www.bookshaker.com* for helping me bring this book to fruition. Thank you to the fabulous friends and clients who've been in my life over the last few years.

And the biggest thanks of all go to my beautiful children for making me happier than I ever thought possible and to my husband Simon - my soulmate, childhood sweetheart and best friend.

Praise for Nadine's Advice

"The book is crammed full of really helpful tips and is heaven sent for a complete novice like me. It is a thoroughly enriching and inspirational read with very clear and easy to understand references. I would thoroughly recommend this to anyone considering making the leap to becoming a VA."

Alison Wright, Co Durham

"The book is a fantastic read with loads of excellent practical things that people can do if they aspire to be a VA. Also I think there is great stuff for everyone, not just VAs. I took note of a few things myself!"

David Slane, Regional Director - Local Business, Barclays

"I am a new VA and feel that this book was written just for me. It is so open and honest and points out many mistakes that I was unaware of, even after completing a recognised VA diploma. Nadine has given me such good ideas about how to focus on my niche and I have found her book very useful."

Sharlene Smith, VA, www.e-virtuality.co.uk

"Although I'm not in the VA business I found the book easy to understand, written with a clear, friendly writing style."

Catherine Gregory, Senior Career Development Adviser, University of Bradford

Introduction

When I started my business, The Dream PA, I was one of the first VAs (Virtual Assistants) in the Yorkshire area. I had originally intended to be a 'freelance VA' – working from home supporting several small businesses and choosing my own hours. I wanted freedom over my schedule and a work life balance. Little did I know that I'd end up creating a formal business, employing staff and renovating a property to become an office for this growing enterprise – a new way of working in an emerging industry!

When I started, there was nothing else like my business to emulate. There was no 'model' in existence for a business that supported other businesses in this way, virtually. The nearest example was that of a temping agency, but I didn't 'send anyone out' to do work on site, as my clients didn't have 'sites'! My clients all worked from home as I did, so in creating The Dream PA, I was effectively writing the blueprint for a new way of working. I'm not saying that what I've done is the only way to run a VA business, but it's the way I have developed, through trial and error, to find a successful formula that suits me. However the beauty of being a Virtual Assistant is that you can create the kind of business you want, to suit your schedule and your own boundaries – It's as flexible as you want to make it! It's only the affordability and accessibility of broadband technology in the UK that makes this kind of 'new working arrangement' possible at all and it's such a new area that there aren't many places to go for information.

'A small business that supports small businesses' is what The Dream PA has become, although it took me the best part of 18 months to arrive at this simplicity. I brought the elements that a small business needs for support under one roof in an affordable way, to allow Sole Traders the kind of executive level support that previously only corporations could enjoy. I started off doing administrative work for a few clients, but when I kept being asked if I could answer their phone as well I started to look for a way to allow me to do this at a price that my clients could handle. The result was my Virtual Receptionist service that puts a full time Receptionist on their business phone-line for just 10p an hour and it is now my most popular service. However business wasn't always this clear cut.

I started off trying to be all things to all people – classic mistake! By saying I could assist anyone – from a Sole Trader to a large company who just wants outside help on a project basis, I assisted no-one. My marketing message wasn't clear enough to appeal to large companies who could always use a temping agency if they wanted help, and saying that I can assist anyone from small to large business just put off the small businesses who perceived that this meant 'expensive'. After all, if a large company can afford this kind of help what chance does a growing one-man band outfit have, for whom cash flow is tight and who is desperately trying to get their own business established and into a flow of regular work?

With such a new industry I searched high and low for advice, guidance and assistance, of which there was little. In a growing market everyone is in the same boat - learning together - which is why I decided to write this book. I wanted to provide a guide to how to get started, what kind of questions to ask and who to ask them of – the kind of help I wish I'd had when I was at the start of my business.

Being a VA is a fantastic way to have a career (without the restrictions and politics that come with large companies) and to combine this fulfilling role with a family balance - whether that means caring for young children or having time for your other hobbies. The downside however, is that the kind of self promotion, boundary setting and supreme confidence that is required to gain and retain clients, doesn't come easy to people like us, who spend their time happily in the background, just getting on with it. We might keep the wheels of daily business turning at our employed jobs and people know that they couldn't accomplish what they did without our strong, reliable help, but openly 'trumpet tooting' about our achievements and how we keep things motoring ahead calmly whilst all around us there's chaos, doesn't feel natural. PAs, secretaries and administrators are largely great 'number twos' - excellent at support, a levelheaded sounding board and a 'rock' to the people we assist. However in this industry, we not only have to be all of that, but also an entrepreneur in our own right, as we are out there trying to win business, gain clients' confidence and establish ourselves as VAs. And that's before we get to the 'doing the work' part!

In this book I'm not going to tell you how to get a website, the legal requirements for setting up a business or how to act at a networking meeting - other 'starting in business' books will cover all of that. This is a practical guide to the unique challenges of starting up as a VA in the UK. You will find if you do further research, that lots of 'Real Estate' agents in the USA use VAs to book their advertising, administer their paperwork and organise their diary. I've tried all routes to market and I've yet to take on one Estate Agent as a client! Therefore this book is written for the British market, acknowledging our unique culture and working practices. I hope that it will provide you with a starting point of how to develop your business from here, provide some new ideas and help you to create something that not only 'does the job' but also suits your preferred lifestyle. After all, that's what being a VA is all about.

So What Exactly Is A VA?

Virtual Assistants (or 'VAs' for short) are the latest buzzword in modern working. Completely unheard of just 20 years ago, the first VAs worked in the USA, Canada and Australia where they were often referred to as 'Home Based Secretaries'[1]. In the early 1990s when the internet was gaining popularity with mainstream businesses and email was becoming commonplace, the term 'Virtual Assistant' was coined and this new industry was born! The first British Virtual Assistants started working from home about ten years ago but it is just within the last five years that this new way of working has really started to gain momentum.

A VA is a remote worker. They often work from their own home, but unlike a tele-worker who is employed by a company but works from home or in the 'field', a VA is self-employed with a variety of different clients to serve. The Virtual Assistant can and will do many different kinds of task, including secretarial work, personal assistance/administration, book-keeping, telephone answering, event or conference organising and virtual office management or co-ordination. Now the role has started to grow to encompass other services that can be done on a remote basis too, which can also include marketing activity and website design and maintenance. Not all VAs will be able to do all of these tasks nor may they want to, but VAs now can pick and choose the services that they will offer, tailoring their VA practice to meet their strengths whilst serving their target clients.

Many VAs will work from home which is a great way to combine work and their other commitments such as family, but VAs can also go to their clients' place of work (even if this is the clients' own home!) or they can work from office premises – often renting out space in a business incubation unit or local business park. The fact that they are 'virtual' doesn't mean that the client never sees them (but it can mean this in some cases!) but just that the VA isn't sat at a desk right outside their office – just as they might be located in a traditional office environment. The VA can have face-to-face meetings with the client, telephone briefings, communicate by email or even have a virtual meeting via webcam if geographical distance prohibits a physical meeting. Some clients are happy for their Virtual Assistant to get on with their tasks and report back when the work is done, some clients like a daily progress report, it's entirely individual and each VA has to find out the clients' preference.

The main thing to note is that trust and competence are extremely important when you are a VA or for a client when they are hiring a VA, because the remoteness of the working arrangement means that the client needs confidence in the person they have appointed to assist them – both that they have the ability to do the work and that they won't fabricate the hours worked or cut corners. Fortunately, most VAs are professionals and act as such, and it is up to the client to do their 'due diligence' when hiring a Virtual Assistant. But in order to have the best chance of securing the client in the first place it is worthwhile for you as the Virtual Assistant to acknowledge the clients' possible fears by assuring them of your competence and having a decent 'Terms & Conditions' statement in place.

BIG OR SMALL?

This is often the question that prospective VAs ask when doing their research about becoming a VA. "What kind of businesses can I support?" The great thing about this new industry is that VAs are not limited to one kind of working arrangement. You could be a Virtual Assistant for a large company or a 'one man band' and in my career I have chosen to support small businesses – the Sole Traders and Partnerships. I chose the 'micro' businesses as there are millions of them to market to and also because that way I get to deal with the business decision maker, and together we can make things happen a lot quicker than can happen when there are layers of management involved. The VAs that I know who have worked with larger companies have taken on these clients as a result of actually working there – they gave up their jobs at the firm then immediately took them on as their first client! This is an extremely slick way of working as they already know the clients' preferences and it takes the worry out of finding that all important 'first client'. The majority of Virtual Assistants that I know of have aimed their services at the SME market (Small and Medium sized Enterprises) because these companies are busy enough to have overflow admin work to outsource but small enough to not have much resource 'In house', making it a perfect fit!

Because Virtual Assistants are professional business people in their own right they charge an hourly rate (plus expenses) to complete their clients' tasks, and this rate can seem high when you work out what the annual salary would be if you worked your old job hours at that rate! However Virtual Assistants are not employees and don't get the 'perks' that employed support staff would expect, such as holiday pay, a pension scheme, share options, professional training or even a desk to sit at! The hourly rate charged needs to cover all of this plus an element for tax and National Insurance payments, because the VA will have to pay their own Self Assessment tax return – there is no longer a 'payroll' team to work this out for you!

On the flipside, VAs are attractive to small businesses precisely for this reason. The small business owner can get their business support tasks completed by a professional, competent executive without having to negotiate the red tape of employment and all that it entails (such as devising employment contracts and ensuring that they are complying with Health & Safety requirements). They simply 'pick up and put down' the VA help as they need it - it is completely flexible, there is no ongoing commitment and it is a way of working that moulds to their own business peaks and troughs. It is a cost effective solution to their work overload, and once a business has used a VA many wonder how they managed before!

For the Virtual Assistant, this way of working involves a lot of juggling, you need to be super organised, but it is a great deal of fun. You might have half a dozen clients on the go at any one time and it can call upon all your patience and diplomacy skills when several of them all want you to do a job for them immediately, but the sheer variety of clients and sense of accomplishment you get when all the plates are nicely spinning is worth getting out of bed each day for!

The main reason that most VAs cite for starting up in this business is that they wanted freedom. Whether you term it 'control', 'flexibility', 'autonomy', 'power', 'liberty', 'opportunity' or 'independence' – it is the same principle – VAs want to:

- Have the power to work the hours they choose
- Be free of the 'office politics' that govern a lot of businesses
- Be able to take a greater part in family life
- Test themselves and their abilities
- Achieve personal growth
- Work in a comfy tracksuit!
- End the long daily commute
- Not spend money on work clothes, cappuccinos and the other knickknacks associated with office working
- Try something new
- Work on their own terms whilst making money
- Be in control of their own destiny!

When it's termed like that, doesn't it sound fabulous?

Fabulous it is but don't confuse 'fabulous' with 'easy'. This is an industry that has grown rapidly over the past few years, so much so that at four years trading my business is widely considered as a 'veteran' in this field, rather than a 'spring chicken'. The Government's criteria for what is an 'established' business is one that has been going for 3 years or more[2] but as the Virtual Assistance industry is still emerging in Britain there are few VAs that have been going even this long.

It is excellent news for anyone looking to start in business as a VA because there is so much opportunity around and the market is on the up. Depending on whether you look at this in a positive way or negatively, there is no 'rule book' for the trade; much of the commercial activity that we as VAs undertake is largely a 'blank sheet' – we are writing the rules as we go along. What I mean by this is that of course we are working to certain professional standards and clients wouldn't hire us if they couldn't see the value in the work we do, but as there isn't much of an occupational history there is no framework to follow.

If we want to expand our business and hire staff we can get standard legal advice on how to do it, but a lot of business support agencies aren't geared up to advise on the unique characteristics of working for clients who cannot see you or of managing staff when you don't have an office. A local business advisor that I saw at the start of my business was a gentleman of advanced years to put it politely, and he couldn't understand how my 'little typing business' (which is how he saw it!) could grow its operation and potentially franchise itself in the future. He just couldn't get his head round the possibilities that a virtual and completely portable business could have. His only frame of reference was to think about the wives of tradesmen who will do their book-keeping and type their letters because the husband is busy installing boilers or erecting scaffolding!

LEGISLATION?

Some VAs can be concerned about the fact that there is, as yet, no 'governing body' who qualify and regulate Virtual Assistants. This seems to be a concern of VAs rather than clients in my experience, as I've observed VA conversations in chat-rooms and had conversations with VAs who have commented about it to me. They would 'feel' better if they could put official VA qualifications next to their name or show membership to an officially recognised organisation. Conversely, in my career so far I have assisted upwards of 100 clients – all business decision makers in their own right, and not one has asked about my VA qualifications. They have bought my ability to do the job and fortunately were proved right when I delivered the work. They did not demand upfront 'proof' of my credentials.

A similar modern vocation to being a VA in this way is coaching. Life Coaches, Business Coaches, Executive Coaches, Personal Performance Coaches, Parent Coaches, Spiritual Coaches etc... This is a field that has rapidly expanded in recent years and started to see a 'boom'. Coaching is not a licensed or regulated industry the way that a profession like the Law is, although in the UK The Coaching Academy[3] is a private business that is leading the way to setting a professional standard for 'best practice'. So far in the history of coaching there hasn't been a supervisory body to oversee them or others working in this area and it hasn't held them back – and the same can be said of our industry.

CONFUSION?

In a growing market the challenges faced by VAs include the usual direct competition, but also actual awareness of what VAs are amongst their potential clients and how a VA can help them. When I first started out, I would be asked "How can you answer my phone if you are not in my office?" by a business owner who didn't realise that phone lines can be diverted to any location. I've had a man in civil engineering demand to know how I can open the post and do the office filing, because he didn't understand that I assist clients virtually on a project basis. Of course in his profession he would have detailed Architects plans posted to him that would need archiving so it was a valid question, but it just highlights how some businesses are easier to support remotely than others!

Once you can accurately define your offer as a VA and succinctly put this across to people you meet at networking events or business meetings, the sometime initial confusion of 'are you a Recruitment Company' will pass! Each new VA will have to decide the area they plan to market to and learn how to educate people about the industry in the simplest way possible and at least whilst they are doing this they are cementing their own expertise in the mind of the listener, creating a possible future client. I find it useful to describe the kind of businesses I support rather than what I actually DO when I'm meeting people who have never heard of VAs. To explain that my clients are "'one man bands' who work from home and I assist them with work for which they pay me by the hour" seems to help them catch on and then their next comment is very often, "What a great idea for a business!" To which I always agree!

CULTURAL DIFFERENCES

In countries outside the UK, it is widely accepted to use a VA to assist with the routine tasks that you could do yourself in business, but that you don't have time to or choose not to. In a country with a more established pattern of outsourcing, VAs are an accepted port of call for businesspeople who need extra help, and the fact that they can pay by the hour for the help they receive makes it a cost effective way of getting things done. The UK by comparison, has a very different work culture to other countries which is why it was necessary to write this book – the first published guide for Virtual Assistants in the UK, written by a British VA. In such a new industry, Virtual Assistants of the future need to hit the ground running and the best way to do this is to arm themselves with information from established VAs who have nursed their battle scars and already learned the most effective ways to do things, what works and what doesn't.

The working culture in this country has the population seemingly programmed to work long hours and to physically do everything themselves. A good VA will be able to gently guide their harassed client into workload delegation and away from the traditional model of 'line of sight' labour whilst ensuring that productivity is maintained. If you have ever worked in an office environment you will know that being able to see someone working does not actually mean they are really 'working' and thus being virtual without the usual office distractions can mean that work is completed in a faster, more focused way.

With more individuals set to launch and run new businesses each year their need for support will grow making it a fruitful stomping ground for Virtual Assistants. The UK Government launched an Enterprise Strategy[4] in March 2008 to boost the UK's enterprise skills and actively support businesses to start up and grow. Couple this with the current world economic climate which means that companies everywhere are looking for cost effective ways to do things in the future and you can see the ongoing potential for 'freelance' help such as Virtual Assistants. Outsourcing is becoming more commonplace and is certainly a way companies can work 'smarter' in the future making it a great outlook for people entering this business. One piece of advice on this note is to steer clear of people who don't immediately see the value of using a VA as these people will be the ones who are most likely to haggle on price, pay late and take your efforts for granted. There are certainly enough of the former business owners around to make a decent living from as a VA.

The next chapter will start to focus your thoughts on what you personally want to achieve from being a VA and how to get started.

What Kind Of Life Do You Want & How To Get Started...

One thing I've observed first hand from working as a Virtual Assistant supporting small businesses, is that many people set up a business in the first place because they are great at their 'job' and want to do this for themselves rather than earn a company money – plus they want more flexibility. However being great at their job doesn't make them natural business people, so rather than working 'on' their business, they work 'in' their business – doing everything themselves and running themselves ragged in the process! Business skills are something that can be learned, so this isn't a barrier to setting up a business, but you should be aware of the tendency of some business owners to fail to relinquish control of every minute detail of the running of their business - ending up with the business running them; and ensure you don't fall into that trap.

In order to create the kind of business and therefore life that you actually want, you need to start with the end in mind. My motivation for starting out on my own was having my first child. I had previously worked long hours in a corporate culture but after having my baby I found my priorities had changed and I no longer wanted to be away from her for 8+ working hours a day and still have an hourly daily commute on top of that! I wanted more freedom and longer term I wanted to be able to do the school run when she began her education.

Being great at organisation was and still is one of my strengths, and when I read a magazine article about a woman who had previously worked as a PA in the office world but had become a VA working from home, this was my 'A-ha' moment! I decided that I could do that and I started to build up a business plan and develop ideas and a name for my new venture in my free time with the plan being to quit the day job when I had secured enough clients to make the business work.

In practice it didn't quite work out this way! I managed to choose my business name and secure the web domains and I worked with a friend who built my website. I wrote all the website content and also created my business Terms & Conditions and various templates such as for timesheets and letters. All of this was done whilst I was also employed and I'd even taken a couple of days holiday from my employer to go to business networking events and start to market my business. However, it was getting tough to devote 100% to my business whilst still being 100% on form in my paid job. I, like many VAs, am conscientious by nature – this is a reason why VAs often do very well once they have learned how to 'sell' themselves to prospective clients; because they know their stuff and will make heaven and earth move to deliver on a clients' expectations. But trying to put 100% into both avenues wasn't working – the maths didn't add up! It was my 'make or break' moment; I could either remain in my reasonably secure, rather dull job that gave me certain perks including a pension, share options and a company car. Or I could commit fully to my new but untested business. The business where I had no idea if it would pan out, but a gut feeling deep down that it just might. The business that I had created from nothing and had just started assisting two clients; I didn't want to let them down but I also had no guarantees that they would remain with me long term. I wasn't making enough money from these two clients to survive and it felt like I was about to leap off a cliff. My stomach was fluttering with bigger nerves than I've ever felt before or since, but I'd tasted the future and wanted to grab hold of it with both hands. I went into work one morning and handed in my resignation, giving one months' written notice. My immediate manager tried to talk me out of it, but my decision had been made and I immediately felt lighter and free.

I had previously booked a weeks' holiday in Scotland before handing in my notice and the timing meant that I would serve out my month at work then that weekend head off for a weeks' break before returning to... no job! I was bad tempered in the car all the way up to Scotland – a good 5+ hours' drive and it was my nerves at the enormity of what I'd done manifesting itself. My husband gently coaxed out of me what was wrong and I had to admit that in all honesty, even though I just knew I'd made the right decision, I was sh***ing myself! (Pardon my language but this phrase is necessary to show my true feelings on the situation!)

After talking a little and putting my fears aside to enjoy the holiday I returned after the weeks break to the serious business of getting some work in, earning some money and learning how to 'do' being a Virtual Assistant. When you are sat at your desk in the quiet with the phone *not* ringing, it's easy to ask yourself, "what on earth have I done?" When you don't want to turn any income producing business away, it's really easy to accept any kind of work because it's a 'job' however it can quickly mean that you end up 'stuck' in a pattern of doing a particular type of work or having a certain kind of arrangement that can be hard to get back out of once a precedent has been set.

PLANNING AHEAD

It is so important to plan out how you want your business to be *before* you embark upon the venture full time. It can be tricky to project your thoughts into the future to map out how your business will look without having experienced what it is like working for a client, and our plans for our businesses naturally change over time with increased knowledge, economic circumstance and what our marketplace dictates. However if you can have an idea of the basics of how you are prepared to work, it will help you to develop a strong offer that will see you in good stead when you are a bit busier and have several clients on the go. One of the basics that you might be firm about is how and where you will complete the work you do for clients.

One of my VA friends started her business at around the same time as me and found that one of her clients wanted her to go into their offices to work, as they didn't really grasp the concept of a VA working from home. She agreed because she didn't want to turn the work away, but it gradually went from 2 days' work a week to whole weeks when they had staff absences, and she ended up basically working a full time position with them without the benefits of being an employee (such as paid holidays and company perks, as she was a 'sub contractor'). Everything was in the company's favour and it took my friend a while to turn this situation around so that she could take on other work and still do her work for this firm from home without losing them as a client. They still have her on site regularly, but at least now this is balanced with her off-site work and she has reached a compromise she is happy with.

BOUNDARIES

When I started out, I would always tell prospective clients that because I'm 'Virtual', the work is done from my home office, rather than me travelling to theirs. I had decided that because my motivation for starting up the business had been to work flexibly from home, then I should always work from home. There was no point in swapping one commute for another. However once I had got a few clients on the go and started to relax a bit, I found that it wouldn't hurt to travel to a clients' home office if they lived within a 20 minute drive of me and if this is what they really wanted. As long as working 'on-site' with a client didn't take up too much of my working week. If I could balance it out then there would be no point in turning the 'on-site' work away.

This ended up being quite a nice arrangement. Because I had originally been so firm about where I will work, the clients' I'd had until then had become used to working with me in this way and I could complete their work around my own schedule at home. As long as I met their deadlines, they were happy. Another client whom I'd travel to was also happy because it meant she could have me do her typing and data inputting from her own office, which also meant I could do some filing and take the post for her too which really helped her out. The work I did for her was a regular five hours a week, so each Tuesday after dropping off my daughter at nursery, I would go to my clients, work 5 solid hours (I'd take a packed lunch to eat at my desk) then I'd leave and return my days' calls before collecting my daughter.

I could be more flexible as time went on because I had set firm boundaries as to where I would work at the start. If I had agreed to work at every clients' home office from the start, I could have found that my day would be spent travelling to various places and being out of my home all day, which wasn't what I'd wanted. Plus, travelling time is 'dead' time. I have occasionally charged my travelling time at half the hourly rate but mostly clients don't expect or like to be charged for your time taken to get to them, so you are creating pockets of time during your day that you cannot charge for if you travel.

Another thing I've learned to be firm about with clients is the kind of work I will or won't do. When I began, my first client was a man I'd met at a networking event. I was telling everyone that I am a Virtual Assistant and I provide PA & Secretarial services, and this chap asked if I would do cold calling as he needed appointments getting into other larger businesses so he could sell his services. I had no previous experience of cold calling but naively thought 'how hard can it be?' I have a tongue in my head and am fairly confident, it is only really 'talking' to people. So I agreed.

It was a disaster. I worked on this project over a period of about 6 weeks and in all that time managed to get him just 1 appointment in another firm. The process of calling up and being constantly rejected or avoided was soul destroying, and I realised that cold calling is *not* one of my talents - it is definitely a 'sales' skill and I am not a natural sales person! Luckily now I have a wonderful telemarketing firm as one of my clients and they are fantastic at cold calling, so whenever I have this kind of request nowadays I pass their enquiry onto the company who often return the favour by sending new clients my way for my telephone answering service.

The sting in the tail of this 'cold calling story' is that I later found out that the client who had come to me for cold calling in the first place had done so because he saw me as a 'cheap' way to get this work done. He had already approached several telemarketing firms and their hourly rate was much higher than mine, so when I came along he pounced! As a matter of fact, he also negotiated with me on price and got me down by £2 per hour too but that's another story!

EXPERIENCE

This client was definitely a learning curve for me, but I'm glad of the experience. It taught me the importance of setting your boundaries and sticking to them, whether that be on price or on what you are prepared to do. I'm pleased to say that since then I have been firm on pricing and it has not stopped me from getting new clients. Once people know where the boundaries are they will operate quite happily within them if they want what you are offering. So don't be afraid to decide what you are prepared to accept and stick to it, although do remain sensitive to the business climate around you. Raising your prices in a recession may be an incredibly smart move or a really silly one – everything needs testing to ensure that you continue to have a steady flow of business coming in.

Decide upon the life you ultimately want right now so you can create a business that serves your dreams and doesn't consume your life. If you have decided that you don't want to commute to your clients let everyone know that whilst you are happy to have the odd face to face 'catch up' meeting at a convenient location, that the majority of the work you do will be virtual – from your own home or office. If you want to be a freelance temp then this is fine, but it may be easier to register with an agency and have them do the hard work of finding you jobs and giving you the benefit of weekly pay and accruing holiday entitlement whilst they get to chase the client for unpaid bills and negotiate prices!

IS THIS REALLY FOR YOU?

Being a self-employed VA is very different to the support role undertaken in many firms. Whilst in a company support staff below a certain level may just be given their work to get on with and managed on the job, a VA is more like an executive PA/office manager role in that the client won't just lead you and give out the work for you to complete, you will be expected to be a self starter and bring your own experience to the table and offer suggestions to them. As a VA you are a business person in your own right so it's up to you to 'own' that role and be as firm with clients as you'd expect a boss to be with you – you manage each other! If you are looking for a role with little responsibility that you can just do quietly from your own home without having to go and look for new work, then unfortunately this is not it! Be critically aware of your preferences as it's easier to find out that this might not be for you now, rather than later on once you've given up your other means of income.

As with any new start up business, the early months are the hardest and it's commonly reported that a lot of start up businesses will fail within their first 12 months of trading. To get your business off the ground there will be times when you have to work a lot - even if your plan was to have more freedom - as it's often necessary at the start to get things moving. I found that in the early days it was hard because I was trying to become known locally and build up a track record, so there were times when I'd be practically working round the clock! I started at 6am some days to complete 2 hours' work before getting my daughter ready for school, then I'd do the school run and back to the office until 5pm when I collected her and even then if I still had work to do I would get her comfortable at the PC on my other desk and put the CBeebies website₅ on for her to keep busy whilst I finished. After taking a couple of hours off for the evening meal and the bath and bed routine, I'd go back to the office and do a few more hours.

Of course long term this wasn't what I wanted, and it wasn't even all 'paid' work – a lot of that time would be spent writing out my client contracts, creating invoices, doing some marketing to attract more paying clients and organising my book-keeping and business systems. But once you have established your presence and had a few satisfied customers you can build momentum by asking them for referrals or testimonials that you can then use to attract more clients. At times your workload might be 'feast or famine' but it's the same for any small business in the early years and keeping your ultimate end goal in mind helps you to get through these hard times.

Now I have built up a good client base of people who are happy with the service and will actually recommend my services to their contacts so I get new work in this way. I still have to do my own marketing to raise awareness of my work and how I can help but it is a lot easier these days because I have a track record of satisfied clients who will vouch for my work if they are asked. Plus I know what the best ways of marketing are for me – what avenues produce the best results for my particular type of client. Unfortunately there is no short cut to getting to this stage – it is a matter of doing the work, getting out and about to meet people and marketing for new clients, but if you persevere and do a good job you'll get there in the end.

FACING THE FUTURE

A good way to determine what you ultimately want in life so you can shape your business around it is to complete a 'Wheel of Life'. This is a tool used by Life Coaches to help you uncover what parts of your life are of high importance to you and what areas need attention. You draw a circle and section it into 8 equal areas like a sliced 'pie'. You can choose what areas mean the most to you but a good example might be: family, work, friends, money, 'me' time, spiritual, personal development, health. The purpose of this 'wheel' is to see on paper what your life looks like today, so choose a segment of your wheel – such as the 'family' segment to start. If '1' is the centre of the wheel and '10' is the outside edge, rate your 'family' score out of 10. If you feel like you get lots of time with your family, you might be a '9' or '10' in this area and if you get no time, you might be a '2' or '3', so wherever you feel you are on the chart, with '10' being the most ideal score you can get, rate your family segment and draw a line across that segment in the part of the wheel relating to your score.

Then, do this for all the areas of the wheel. When you have finished, you will end up with a visual diagram that shows where the time in your life is being spent now and you can go round the wheel's sections again with a different colour pen if you wish, to mark where you *want* the score to be. The most balanced, ideal life would look like a perfect circle, whereas our own circles might be very uneven. This tool helps us to see what areas need attention and helps us focus on them.

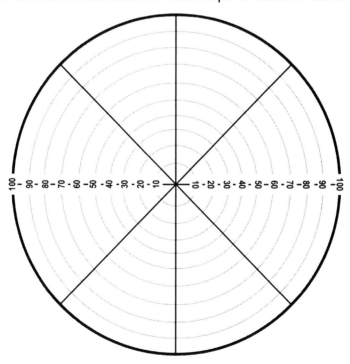

My wheel when I was still in my employed job, showed I was doing great on the 'work/career' and 'finances' sections of the wheel but didn't have as much family time or 'me' time as I would like. My 'health' and 'spiritual' sections weren't that good either! My end diagram showed a very unbalanced wheel but it helped me to focus on where I wanted to improve and what I ultimately wanted from life. When I did a wheel after starting my business, the shape was different once again and every year when I do this exercise the wheel is gradually becoming more rounded. Life will still throw events to dent the wheel in one area from time to time, but ultimately with the wheel, you can keep tracking whether you are 'on course' for the life you want and it is only from knowing this that will help you define and shape your business.

PRACTICALLY SPEAKING...

Now you have given some thought to how you want your business to eventually be, what are the practical steps and tools that you need to get started?

Setting up your office is both exciting and often expensive but you don't need to be 'all singing and dancing' right from the start. The bare minimum that any new VA needs to operate is:

- a PC or laptop computer (ideally with a printer)
- a phone number (a landline or a mobile)
- a quiet and safe place to concentrate and store any files (even if this is a corner of your bedroom until you really get going)
- some business cards

Items such as filing cabinets, laminators, white boards, stock of stationery, fancy brochures of your services and your website can be created and included within your business when time and finances allow. Once you have money coming in you will probably want to 'upgrade' the things you bought early on in your business anyway, so there is no point in spending a lot of money at the outset. Also, the technology changes so swiftly and you may end up working with clients in ways that you couldn't have imagined at the start, so items that you think you need may just gather dust. A good tip is to wait until a job demands a certain piece of equipment before you rush out and buy it. Learn from one of my mistakes! My four ring hole punch has never been used and I've only ever used my CD labelling kit once. Most of my clients prefer their work sending digitally in a Word Doc, PDF or MP3 format, so to stop it going to waste my stock of blank CDs was used to make my own computer file back-ups in the early days before I found more effective software.

MAKE IT EASY

What's important is to pay attention to 'the basics'. To attract paying clients you will need to make it as easy as possible for them to buy from you. Part of this involves making it easy for them to reach you first of all! On your business cards you will want your name, company name, your address (It's ok to put your home address – many small business owners do), your email address and your telephone number. Having a fax number isn't essential nowadays and if you think your clients will want one, you can download low cost 'fax to email' software from the internet which will give you a fax number to put on your cards then any faxes sent to you will arrive in your Inbox as an email attachment.

You will need to carry your business cards on you all the time as you never know when an opportunity to hand one out will come along! It is expected that you will have a business card when you attend a business networking event, and if you don't have one with you there might just be another VA there who does, so don't miss out on any opportunities. The potential client will go with the assistant who appears more prepared.

As for computer software, it is likely that you will need:

- a basic word processing package on your PC
- along with the ability to work with spreadsheets
- email software
- and an internet browser as a minimum.

Over the years I have added all kinds of extras such as speech recognition software, audio recording software, a webcam, Skype₆, PDF convertors and book-keeping software, but the basics that I use every day are the former four items.

Once your 'office' is kitted and ready you should start to get your systems in place before taking on any clients. Being prepared in advance will help you to portray a more professional first impression to your prospective clients, and thinking about this aspect of business and sorting it out before you start means you can forget about it once you become occupied with fee earning tasks, so it's a better use of your time to do it now.

SYSTEMISE

The best way to stay organised when you are juggling multiple clients, each with differing priorities and staggered deadlines is to ensure that your systems are watertight, so that even when they don't know what to do next, you always know where you are.

One of the main things you will need to organise is the tracking of your time so you know what to charge clients. There is software available to buy on the internet whereby you create a record for each client then 'punch a virtual time-clock' when you start and end on their work and it works out the time spent on each client each month for billing, but my advice is to keep it simple.

The system I use is paper based and involves a simple timesheet[7]. I have a separate foolscap wallet for each client with their contact information on the front and inside the folder is their timesheet. I record the date and start time when I begin their work and note the end time when I complete their work. Then whatever time I work is rounded up or down to the nearest 5 minutes. For example, 1 hour 27 minutes would be logged as 1 hour 25 minutes but this is only because I charge my clients in advance. When I invoiced clients *after* I had done the work, I would round the time *up* to the nearest 15 minute interval. I will explain more about my billing system later. Alongside the time logged for each client is a brief list of the tasks I did for them that day. This way if a bill is ever queried by the client I can give them a break-down of where the time was spent.

The folder system for managing each client is really simple and it works. I also have a file set up on my PC for each client and I put copies of all the work I do for them on there too so I can easily email it to them or refer back to what we did several months ago. However the fact that I always have a 'paper' file on each client means I can keep my most current jobs for them in there so I know immediately what we are working on, and it is completely portable if I need to work on their jobs outside of my office or if we have a meeting off-site.

FORMALITIES

Many new VAs that I meet ask if I get my clients to sign a contract when we start working together, and if so, "what should they put in their contract?" Whilst at the very beginning of my work as a VA I did have a contract which I got a couple of clients to sign as time went on I revised this into a statement of Terms & Conditions. I only had a contract at the start because I thought I should, but it hasn't really proved that useful and can even be more off-putting to potential clients in some cases.

You may have heard the expression 'not worth the paper it is printed on'. In my early weeks as a VA I remember asking a lawyer who I'd met about how enforceable these kinds of contracts are. This expression was their reply to me!

I have also noticed that some Virtual Assistants have put their contracts onto their websites including statements about how they will charge interest on late payments and how they require briefing before 5.30pm to complete a job by a certain date. Whilst I can support their need to be firm and have boundaries, I don't agree with broadcasting it in this way. Until they have got the client on board and have actually done some work with them, the client will not know if this assistant is worth all the hassle and may decide not to use them. A formal contract often puts working practices into your own terms and they are included for your own convenience, whereas what a potential client wants to know is how YOU can help THEM. This is what you need to address rather than how you will be treating late payers, so a Terms & Conditions statement is an alternative, friendly way to show your professionalism whilst instructing the client towards your preferences.

Once you have created your vision for the business and formalised your working systems the next step is to think about where your clients will come from. To do this you should consider what specialist skills you have or the areas you'd prefer to work in and attract clients that fit with your strengths. The next chapter explores this in more detail.

What Is A Niche, Why Is It Important & How Do You Find It?

People enter the VA profession from all kinds of backgrounds and a variety of different industries which means that they all have unique talents. However a common direction for a lot of new VAs to take is to promote themselves as a 'general Virtual Assistant' to all the available markets, in the false belief that it will get them more work. I tend to disagree.

As we all know, businesspeople are busy, they have little time (which is why they need us!) but it also means that they don't have the time or patience to work out how you may be able to assist them. As the VA it is up to us to spell it out for the potential client and the best way to do this is to be specific.

In everything we say and everything we do, we need to show the clients out there that we are their natural choice. Consider what will make your potential client think, "I've come to the right place". The best way to do this is to think of the person you want to make one of your clients and address their needs directly.

When I wrote the content for my website *www.thedreampa.co.uk* I wanted the target client to know at a glance that this was a business that could help them – particularly with their telephone answering. I have tweaked sentences and words over the years as the business has evolved, but one of the main things that I did was to put bullet points on the homepage to draw the readers' attention to exactly what need it is that I have the solution for. If the person reading my site can answer 'Yes' to my question, then they will see that I can definitely help their business. If they cannot answer 'Yes' to the question I pose, then I might possibly be able to help them but it would involve further discussion.

However the aim both on my website and when I am speaking to potential clients, is to 'cut to the chase' as quickly as possible. To let the client know that I have a service that will help their business to grow and as there are plenty of business-people who can answer 'Yes' to my question which is "Are you running a business as a sole trader, freelancer, consultant, partnership or small Limited company?" then I don't bother trying to market to the people whose answer is 'No'.

MARKET TO A NEED

I chose to market my business to other small businesses which is the way I am specific in my own marketing. Within the term 'small business' there are a million different industries but I am not marketing my services at a certain industry as such, I am marketing toward a specific need which is their need to have their incoming calls answered. If I am marketing my admin support toward particular industries then I will aim my activity toward the fashion, lifestyle and motor industry as these are fields that I have worked in and have plenty of experience in – these are my natural clients for this kind of virtual assistance work and this is what I mean by a niche.

Telephone answering is one of the services that I offer through my business and I do this alongside my administrative support work. Admin time is charged to clients at an hourly rate which means that I can only possibly assist one client at a time. However, through my Virtual Receptionist service₈ that I purchased as a franchise to 'bolt on' to my business, I can support many clients at the same time and be earning from each of them, so this side of the business is scaleable – but it is a 'numbers game'. In order to earn decent money from this service I need to have plenty of clients on board, so I go after Virtual Receptionist clients at the same time as completing my other fee earning work, marketing for them both in tandem which is also a good way of spreading my risk across the whole business. If one type of work dries up temporarily I still have another avenue to go down until I can replace any 'lost' clients so the whole business keeps on moving ahead.

BE SPECIFIC

I am very clear in my mind about the kind of clients that I can attract for each side of the business and because I 'know' this type of client so well, I know what their issues are, what keeps them awake at night and what the service is that they need – so I can market to it. By being specific I can assist more people because I have an obvious message about whom I can help and I can say it explicitly enough for the recipient of the message to quickly grasp, "She's talking about me!" It is by being specific that clients can more easily see how I can assist them, so I get more enquiries for new work than if I had simply stated what I DO and expected the recipient to figure out how that would work for THEM.

To hit upon the formula that's right for you and find your own niche, you will need to excavate your hidden talents and realise their value. Most of us tend to think our skills are 'nothing special' until we get out of our comfort zone and look around at what other people do in business and the ways they describe their own strengths. I used to take my 'marketing head' for granted, thinking it was patently obvious to everyone how to define a product or service with clarity so it could be widely understood or what the best way to get in front of my potential customers would be. Until I started speaking to other small business owners.

I quickly discovered that it is something that is not obvious to everyone and that I had a 'hidden' talent, which meant that I could also define one of my business niche areas as being able to support small businesses with aspects of marketing. I didn't want to become a marketing agency or to exclusively do marketing work, but it was something special that I could bring to the table to assist my clients in a way that many other VAs couldn't, so this became my niche and a way to attract clients whilst setting myself apart from the competition.

FIND YOUR HIDDEN TALENTS

Maybe your background is in the legal field. Legal secretaries have skills and knowledge that more general administrators don't have, so your niche might be to support small businesses in the legal area or perhaps 'Virtual HR professionals'. You will have an appreciation of the factors that this audience has to consider when assisting their own client base and therefore knowledge of how you can adequately support this. You'll have a basic understanding of common legal terms and your history in this field provides a track record making it easier to win clients in the first place.

If charity work is your thing, then you might position yourself as an assistant to help your clients with fundraising and applying for grants, having an understanding of the complexities of the funding systems.

If you are bi-lingual, your niche could be to assist entrepreneurs in both the UK and the other country that you can communicate with! There is no end to the possibilities of who your niche could be, but having a firm area to market your services to will focus your attention on communicating in an uncomplicated way to this sector and your message will be more widely heard and understood.

JUST AN ASSISTANT?

Some VAs find it difficult to define their niche so that they can set themselves apart from other VAs who are in the 'general practitioner' category. VAs who say they are 'just an assistant' need to think about what exactly they brought to the roles they have worked in the past. Break down the tasks done and what that actually meant to the business you worked for - you may be surprised at the amount you actually did, whilst taking your organisational and task completion skills for granted.

Many entrepreneurs out there are great 'ideas people' but often lack the discipline to 'follow through'. If you are a 'finisher - completer' then your drive, structure and attention to detail will be highly appreciated by a more disorganised but equally passionate worker who needs the push to get things done. This could be your niche – the Project Manager or 'details' person. Whatever you decide, bear in mind that people like the security of dealing with an 'expert' in their particular situation and when you define a niche you are taking on expert status in that field.

Think about it, would you rather take baby advice from your mechanic or your midwife? It's the same with the VA industry!

GETTING HELP

In my experience and from what I have observed, many fledgling VAs might ask other VAs for advice, both directly and on internet VA forums. These forums are a great way to get peer support and to find out how other VAs are feeling - they can also give you an idea of how busy another Virtual Assistant is. You can often pick up tips on what software others are using and find out about the kind of work that VAs are being asked to do.

However this isn't the most effective way to source assistance in helping you to define your niche. Firstly, the 'competition' element is there and even if you do find out about their business and how they market for clients you are learning the best way to get a carbon copy of someone else's business – and what good is that? Know what others do by all means, but then do it differently. From the clients' point of view, if you are the same as everyone else then why should they come to you? What will you do for them that is special? If the answer is 'nothing' then you may find it a slow, uphill struggle to get off the ground.

Use VA forums by all means, but don't take everything said on them too literally. A lady who is exploring the possibility of becoming a VA recently called me to ask for advice and commented how everything she'd read on the VA forums was 'doom and gloom'. From reading the comments it gave the impression that there is no work out there – no paying clients and times are hard. Whilst I'm sure that this is the reality for the individuals who are posting comments on the forums, it is not necessarily the reality for all Virtual Assistants.

Consider that many successful VAs who are juggling fee paying clients and growing their businesses don't necessarily have the time to participate regularly on forums as they are too busy with their clients! The VAs that I know who are well established also don't feel the need to visit these forums regularly because being on them does not actively bring in new clients. It is merely a way to communicate with your VA peers and whilst it is nice to tap into the general discussions every once in a while, participating in them is not going to help your business grow. Your time could be spent on marketing your business.

Forums can be a good way to market yourself to potential clients, but consider the audience wisely. Forums that are used by small businesses in general (not specific to VAs) are a fairly good way to inexpensively get your business name out there and showcase some of your expertise which might be instrumental in attracting a new client. So don't shy away from forums, but take VA specific forums with a pinch of salt. After all, would other VAs be your target market for fee paying clients?

ASK YOUR POTENTIAL CLIENTS

The very best way to develop your business, find your niche and make sure that you are giving paying customers the services that they want is to ask them! This sounds simple, but surprisingly underused! Think about the kind of work you'd like to do, then focus on whom you would need as a client to do this kind of work, then look at your immediate circle to see who you know who fits this profile. If you don't know anyone, then look at who in your circle does and ask for an introduction.

Once you have a few potential contacts in mind, tell them you are researching businesses like theirs as you want to develop an offer to assist them and businesses like them. Devise a short questionnaire to help you capture the information about what their immediate support need is so you can ensure that you address that need in your marketing. Your aim is not to convert them into one of your paying clients, but to get honest information out of them so be careful that you don't appear like you are 'selling' to them. It will simply put them off and you won't get any good facts out of them. What you are looking for is to use the information they give you to help you go after other businesses like theirs and convert these into clients, using a more focused and targeted way.

As lifestyles are increasingly busy and people are pushed for time, this is both a blessing and a curse to the startup VA. The frantic lifestyle of many businesspeople means that assistance of some kind is needed and welcomed – if the price is right, but it also means that getting a spare 10 minutes out of someone to get the information you need may be difficult. One way to sidestep this problem is to offer them something free in return for their information - you will get their full attention and more importantly, honest feedback.

If you are interested in assisting small companies then offer the owner manager of a business like this a free 'efficiency audit'. Everyone likes to get something for free and by offering an audit on their existing systems and procedures, you can identify gaps in their structure that you or a service like yours could fill - its great market research. Most importantly, you will have opened a dialogue with a business owner where you can then ask them for help in return – like their answers to your questionnaire! You may have to be creative in finding ways to get a busy person to spend 10 minutes giving you the information you need, after all, we all tend to steer away from the people on the street with clipboards who ask for a 'minute of your time' when we are trying to get somewhere! But once you have spoken to a handful of people in the area that you are looking to serve then you will have a better idea of what services they actually need and will pay for, and this kind of information will be the lifeblood of your business.

KEEP IT SIMPLE

I remember at the start of my business I was concerned with trying to appear as 'well rounded' as possible and show clients that whatever their administrative need, I could fulfil it. I had a list of the various services that I could do on my website, listed in alphabetical order and it included things like 'book-keeping, confidential typing, data inputting and writing press releases'. However to show that I can help in any way, I also thought it would be a great idea to offer a 'reminder service' (for important diary dates) and a Christmas card writing service to remove that hassle from my potential clients.

I was quite proud with my creativity in coming up with all these great ways in which I could possibly help a future client and I showed my list to a lady who had more than 16 years experience in running her own business (not as a Virtual Assistant – her business was in PR). This lady and I had met at a local networking event and I'd expressed an interest in having a mentor whom I could ask for advice in growing my business and she'd agreed to be my sounding board. Upon reviewing my services list she promptly asked me, "where my head was at?" and told me that the priorities of small business owners are getting new work in and cutting costs – not worrying about their Christmas card list! When it was spelled out to me so bluntly I could see her viewpoint but I was crushed. I had trained my eye on the wrong prize. In trying to offer services that were unique and would set me apart from my competitors, I took my eye off the commercial ball – what people would actually pay for. This 'reality check' was hard to hear at the time but she was absolutely right, and for the next couple of years in business as I learned my own way and my confidence grew, I would ask myself 'how she would handle this' when considering a possible idea for my business, to keep me on the right track.

COMMERCIAL REALITY

It's easy with the novelty of setting up a brand new business venture to let your imagination run wild and decide to offer services that you have always wanted to do or that sound great in principle. Maybe you have sat in your employed position whilst working for someone else, dreaming of the day you set up on your own and would do things your way. It's great to have passion for what you do but always be mindful of the commercial reality. Is there a market who will pay for what you propose to offer? If you are not sure, do some research but always question what you are offering and ensure that it fills a need somewhere. Even if it is not your intention to become a millionaire through your business, you will presumably still need to make money so will need enough paying customers to make that happen.

EMBRACE YOUR LIMITS

In defining your business niche be sure to embrace your limits. You might have a great idea for a potential market for you to serve but within that market you may not be good at or want to do every task that is asked of you. Unlike applying for a support role job where you have to be seen to do every aspect of support work, or where it is expected that you have certain skills, you can choose your own remit when working for yourself.

Therefore if you are a whiz at audio typing then let this be your 'thing'. It is a special hook for marketing and you will become known as *the* person for any audio typing assignments that emerge. Using audio typing as an example, and thinking about the kinds of clients that might need this service more than others, you might decide to target journalists in your marketing, to see if they would like you to transcribe their interviews. I have one VA colleague who assists a journalist on a trade magazine for the knitting and yarn industry. It might not be as glamorous as 'Hello' magazine, but she has several hours of work per month from this client who visits trade shows in the Far East and records interviews, and passes the tapes for her to transcribe upon his return. It is regular work for her and saves him lots of time at the keyboard when he returns from business trips.

By the same token, I have another VA friend who hates audio typing (because of an ex boss who used to record transcription whilst on the loo and other delightful places – but that's another story!) and she never accepts audio work so she uses this preference to define her preferred work parameters. She has the skill to complete audio typing assignments, it's just that she prefers not to, so she passes this work onto another VA near her when she is asked about it. If you are not as good at a particular area or don't enjoy that kind of work, then use this preference to set a boundary around what services you will offer.

NETWORKS

Expanding your network of Virtual Assistants is a good way to help each other by passing work to another VA when you cannot do the job or don't have the capacity at that time. It's always handy to know other VAs in your area and what kind of work they do and it is likely that you will meet these VAs naturally at local business networking events whilst you are going out to promote your own business, so you don't have to spend a lot of time hunting them down!

So now you have an idea of what your potential niche might be and have looked at the needs of the clients you wish to serve, you are ready to start marketing your business to bring in new clients! The next chapter goes into more detail.

How To Make Potential Clients Aware Of Your Business Even If You Don't Know About Marketing

When you launch your business you will need to undertake some heavy marketing activity to get it off the ground. After all, if no-one knows about you, you won't get any clients!

NETWORKING

The quickest way to start the ball rolling is to find out what business networking events there are in your area and go to them! By meeting people face to face you can tell them about what you do and find out about their business, and by listening, you'll hear opportunities for you to help them which means you can promote your services.

You might listen for people saying for example, that they don't have time to get everything done, or that they haven't got around to starting a certain project yet, opening the door for you to tell them what you do and how you could assist them.

No-one wants to be given the 'hard sell', so gently say how you assist other people and they pay you by the hour for as long as they need help with no ongoing commitment. You are letting people know that help is out there if they want it and they don't have to worry about being 'tied in' to some kind of contract. They just 'pick you up and put you down' as they see fit!

I always listen for people who say they are going on a business trip or on holiday, or who have a heavy week of meetings coming up, and I ask them how they will manage their incoming calls during that time. If they have a business with staff, they will most likely be ok and not really need any extra support, but a Sole Trader will usually have no back up in place and they will let calls be taken by their answering machine. I then ask them how many hang up calls they get or if they know how many calls they are missing and this makes them think about the possibility that they are losing business by missing calls.

I never push my service onto anyone but I give them the information on hours of operation, price for the monthly service and the calls and how I can offer a free trial for a one month duration, then I leave it up to them. Some clients take me up on the free trial straightaway and some just thank me and move on, but of the ones who move on, a good few will come back to me at a later date and enquire again then. Not everybody will be in the market for what you are offering at the time you meet them, but if you and your business are of interest to them, they will keep your card and probably follow up later on. I've had calls from people who met me 18 months earlier to ask about the possibility of help, so it takes time but networking is well worth it!

You can find out about business networking events through your local Business Link[9]. This is a Government backed business support service to help start-ups and established businesses and they often have a calendar of events that you can book onto to meet other business in your area. The Chamber of Commerce[10] is another organisation with offices regionally who are there to help businesses to network and grow. There are international networks such as BNI (Business Network International)[11] and BRX (Business Referral Exchange)[12] which are franchised networks that have the specific focus of bringing business people together to network and therefore potentially increase their business. There will also be several privately owned business networking groups in your area. The best way to find out about these groups is to speak to people at the events you attend and ask them what other networking they do? Then you can get the contact details of the organiser and talk directly to them about attending their next meeting.

ONLINE NETWORKING

Networking is a very direct way to reach potential new clients and the benefit is that they can see you for themselves first hand, to decide whether they like you and want to do business with you. But networking is not limited to 'face to face' avenues. You can also join online networking groups and promote yourself through these. The added benefit of these platforms is that you are not limited to a certain time of the day when you can engage in networking activity and you can widen your geographical reach be promoting yourself to businesses outside of your immediate area. This is particularly useful for Virtual Assistants as we can help clients based anywhere in the world!

There are too many online networks to mention here but a few well known ones are Ecademy[13], LinkedIn[14], Ryze[15] and Boss to Boss[16]. There are new networks emerging all the time and also ones with a specific audience such as women (WiRE[17] is one example) so keep your radar up for new opportunities to network and increase your business contacts.

Plus, a lot of these online networks have forums which as I mentioned in the last chapter, is a good 'cost free' way to get your business name and web address 'out there' and seen by business people who might want to use your services. If you don't have a website at the start you can put your email address in there or your phone number, so that anyone reading your comments has a way to contact you if they wish to, but having a website is the best way to showcase your business so do aim to get one as soon as finances allow.

PR

Another way to raise awareness of what you do is to approach your local newspaper to tell them about the launch of your new business. The start of something is a great time to get media coverage and unlike advertising, editorial coverage is free! The Business Editor would be the best person to approach and all you need to do is simply send them a one page 'press release' about who you are and what you do, either by email or in the post.

There is a structure to a press release, but essentially you need to cover the basics: 'who, what, why, where, when and how' and focus on the benefits of your service. For example, "Jane Doe of Leeds has set up a new business" is not very interesting to anyone, but an article about how "local woman Jane Doe is helping other small businesses in the region to compete with larger organisations" is much more attention grabbing. The press release would then go on to say that in response to the high number of start up businesses in the region in the last 6 months/year, Jane Doe launched her VA business to provide 'pay as you go' support to other small businesses, spotting a gap in the market etc, and finish off with a quote from you.

The fact that the virtual assistance industry is so new is a massive bonus in terms of generating media coverage because journalists like to hear about anything different or new. If you were an accountant setting up an accountancy practice this wouldn't be as interesting to the press because it's been done before, so the industry you've chosen puts you in a great position for achieving media attention and therefore free coverage!

Another tip for getting coverage is to send in a photograph with your press release. This makes the story more 'human interest' and they are more likely to give you a larger amount of page space with a photograph attached to your article than without.

It can never be guaranteed that you will be featured and get coverage in the local paper. The only way to guarantee coverage is to pay for it by taking an advert but the costs associated with this are so large for a start up business that is often out of reach. Also, it is widely recognised that editorial coverage is 3 times more effective than advertising because it's more likely to be read and it is seen as 'third party' endorsement to have the paper write about you. The only thing you will have spent if your coverage fails to appear is your time. As a start up business time is one thing you will have more of than when you are further along the road with several clients vying for your attention, so you have little to lose by giving it a go!

DIRECT MARKETING

Marketing your business may be as simple as having a small flyer produced to illustrate what services you provide and then handing this to business people you meet at networking events or posting the flyers through the doors of businesses you are looking to target. You could do a mail shot to businesses you don't know, writing a covering letter and enclosing one of your flyers. Various organisations sell mailing lists of business names and addresses that you might target, examples of places you could go for this kind of information would be Business Link[9] or The Chamber of Commerce[10].

FREE MARKETING

Take every 'no cost' opportunity you can to raise awareness of your business too. In the early days when you have little income from your VA business, you should aim to get known for free wherever you can! Directories such as the 'Yellow Pages' and 'Thomson Local' will provide a free basic listing to your business which often involves being featured in their printed directory and on their website, so take advantage of this opportunity. They will probably call you after you submit your listing to try to 'up-sell' you to taking out a paid advert that would give you a box or allow you to include your web address for example, but you don't have to take them. You can just accept the free listing to have a presence in their book and decline anything else if you want to. Free listings won't usually contain 'enhanced information' such as your web address – you would have to pay to have this included, but it should include your business name, telephone number and address.

Another place to list your business for free that is specific to the Virtual Assistance industry is The Alliance of UK Virtual Assistants[18]. I have had a listing in this directory since the start and have had several enquiries for new business from it. However because it is free and it is run by a small team of volunteers who are also VAs themselves, the listings are added when they have time so it may not be as immediate as you'd get with a 'paid for' listing. Again, if you need to make changes to your listing you could have to wait some time until the change can be made.

Another specific VA directory is the IAVA[19] – The International Association of Virtual Assistants. This group does charge a monthly fee to be listed in their directory but I have never taken a listing so cannot comment on the response rate for being listed.

Explore all the options available to you then choose where to promote your business based on your available budget and where you think your target clients might search for you, but whatever you do, keep the marketing activity up. It's important to be active when marketing your business so potential clients know you are still around, are ready and willing to assist and so they remember you over the other Virtual Assistants out there who are vying for their attention!

NICHE MARKETING

There are lots of ways to make potential clients aware of your business and a particularly effective one is to tie awareness in with the niche you have decided to support. For example, if you decided that you would assist financial service clients, (maybe working exclusively with IFAs or mortgage brokers) you could target their industry publications for coverage, to get yourself directly in front of the businesspeople within your chosen arena.

Each industry has specific needs, so if you were a VA within the financial services sector, then it would be extremely useful to already have a database of the major insurance companies' contact details. Plus they all handle queries and quotes in different ways so knowing each company's preferences would make your job faster and inspire confidence in your IFA client that you understand their industry and can handle their workload. A VA with all this contact information to hand, perhaps on a spreadsheet, will already be one step ahead of a 'general VA' who doesn't specifically understand how the financial sector works. There is also compliance etiquette to follow within financial services and this includes objectives for the IFA such as ensuring that they promptly send out 'Letters of Engagement' to their clients. This is an admin heavy undertaking and the IFA's time could be better spent searching the market for the best deals, rather than doing the routine admin tasks - this is where a VA would come in.

If you were marketing to this niche it could be worth approaching the financial industry publications with an idea for an article on your business – the 'new way of working' that is assisting IFAs all over the country helping them to become more productive. Pitching it as a 'Day in the life of' kind of piece would showcase you as an expert administrator in this field whilst providing a very interesting and informative article for the publication to write for their readers. Plus it would get you in front of a very specific audience of potential clients for your business.

But niche marketing is not limited to publications. Different industries have their own internet forums and you can highlight your business by posting intelligent comments on one of these. As long as you are not overly aggressive in your tactics you can find places that will allow you to advertise yourself and your services without upsetting anyone.

Get to know your target market inside out to find ways to promote yourself within it. You may think that being a 'general VA' will mean that you get more business, but with such a wide range of marketing opportunities to go at, the danger is that you will end up doing nothing or very little. A more targeted approach (niche marketing) will focus your attention and make it easier to track the results of your efforts rather than having dribs and drabs of effort spread everywhere.

All of this activity is considered 'marketing' so even if you have never done any marketing before you can see that it is simply a matter of getting a certain audience to be aware of and think positively about you and your business, and more importantly, informing them of what you can do for them. So be creative with your thinking and use any and every opportunity to do some marketing for your small business.

Each time you reach a business milestone (such as 1st year in business, the launch of a new service that you are offering, or taking on an employee if you ever decide to do this) then consider issuing a press release and photo to your local media to tell them about it. Hopefully they will use your story and give you some free coverage, and a constant drip feed of media articles builds up a great profile over time and lends credibility to your business. Plus, another upside is that when you have been running your business for a while, having media coverage will assure clients that you still plan to be around in a few years' time. This kind of assurance will be important to them if you are building up a relationship and are becoming an integral support in their business – they won't want to suddenly lose you when you have got to the stage where you can anticipate their moves!

CREATIVE MARKETING

Other ways to market your business whilst being creative is to consider offering your service as a 'prize' at a networking event for example. You might run a 'prize draw' to a business for one hours' free book-keeping assistance for example, or half a day's work in their office. Whatever it is, if you are offering a free prize, make sure that the organiser announces your business and what you do to everyone before drawing the prize. The winner will get to try you out for free but the rest of the room will have heard what you do and may be interested enough to ask for your business card afterwards. It's all about getting enough people to hear of you so that a percentage of them will take it further and you will have secured another client.

All of these suggested activities are ways of raising awareness of what you do and can be done at no or low cost. It's up to you to decide what you are comfortable with and how much you want to promote your business and some avenues will have more success than others. I have done all of them in some form, making the offer relevant to my own particular business and I've had results in varying degrees from each tactic, so they can work!

MARKET RESEARCH

Marketing for new business and getting those early clients will be a steep learning curve, but it is necessary to do the groundwork as it informs you about your own business. When you are putting your company name around, you will be approached by people and asked if you can do the job they have in mind. The questions that you are asked can provide a useful insight into what the current market wants and needs and if you feel you can accommodate that within your business, you can easily adapt to the market climate.

The great thing about being the boss of your own small business is that you can adapt quickly and easily to market changes. You can be flexible and almost 'chameleon like' in your ability to cater for your clients and potential clients – you don't have to go through layers of management to get even the simplest initiative signed off! Those of you who have worked for larger companies will know what I mean by this. Sometimes it can be frustrating when you are chomping at the bit to get moving on something and the people who need to give the nod are moving at a snails' pace or don't 'get' what you are trying to do. There is none of this to hold you back when you are running your own business.

When you start to market your own individual business you begin to get an idea about the needs of your potential market and what services they want. You can keep your radar open for feedback and use this to keep your business at the front edge of the market's needs.

Until you have your first client on board, you still have an 'escape clause' if you want it – you can decide to go back to the 'safety' of what you know – the 'security' of your paid employment, without too much risk or upheaval. Upon actually securing your first client, you move into new territory and there is less likelihood of 'going back'. If you are still with me at this stage then you are obviously serious about your VA business and will need to decide what rate you are going to charge for your services. You need to be able to cover the outgoings involved in running your business, take a stipend and make a profit. The next chapter looks at how to make money from your business as a Virtual Assistant, and where to set your hourly rate...

How To Make Money & Set Your Hourly Rate

Pricing is always an area that many new VAs get nervous about. It is likely that this will be the first occasion in the Virtual Assistant's life when they will have had to confidently state their value to a prospective client, not knowing if the client will take it or leave it! It's hard at the best of times to discuss money – our British reserve takes care of that. Plus think back to your last salary negotiation with an employer – we rarely push for what we know we are worth! However setting your rate as a VA is different. This time, you are in the driving seat and whilst you want to be fair with your pricing, you should not fall into the trap of pricing yourself too low, just to get work in.

START WITH THE END IN MIND

Just like you did when deciding what sort of clients you would go after and what your niche market would be, start with the end in mind when it comes to pricing too. What you end up deciding to charge clients will largely depend upon what you want your 'end' business to look like, because it can be tough to move yourself into a new price bracket once your clients have become used to paying a certain rate.

For example, when you sat down and decided to become a VA in the first place, you must have thought about the kind of clients you'd like to work with. If you have skills from a particular sector, this will help determine the kind of offer you promote, and what clients you take on. An Independent Financial Adviser client may be perfectly willing to pay you £25 per hour to do admin work (especially as they can earn approx £150 per hour themselves!) whereas a Painter/Decorator who charges £15 an hour for their own labour will never hire you to do admin at a rate of £25 per hour, so your rate will depend upon the market you wish to serve. Do you envisage yourself assisting trades-people or people in service based businesses?

It's tempting to say you will only assist the 'Professional' businesses such as IFAs, Accountants, Mortgage Brokers etc, who might be more willing to pay a higher hourly rate for your help. These people generate a lot of paper and do need help to control it and it is a good move to 'go where the money is'. However if your skills are not already in this niche, it will probably take you longer to start to attract these kinds of clients because you have to start from scratch.

When looking at the clients you want to work with, some clients will expect you to travel to their offices to do the work because of their own client confidentiality issues, or simply that they physically have too many paper files that need organising to post or bring to you - the work would simply be completed more easily at their own office. This is something we briefly covered before but is particularly worth stating again when looking at the professions that may be happier to pay a larger hourly rate because you will need to decide if the money you could earn would be worth the travelling, if your primary reason for setting up your business was to work from home or have more work life balance.

AVERAGE RATES?

When considering pricing and hourly rates it's good to know what the market average currently is. The typical price range for VAs is between £15 and £25 an hour, although some Virtual Assistants charge less than this and some charge more. A friend of mine who is a VA charges £12.50 per hour for her work as she works only with people locally (not nationally) and she believes that in her area people will not pay more than this for admin support. I can balance this assumption out by letting you know that I operate just over 3 miles away from her and also look after clients locally (as well as further afield) and I successfully charge £25 per hour for admin support and have done for two to three years. I have fewer actual clients on the admin front to serve than she does, but I earn more for the hours I do and personally I would rather do more work with those that pay me what I'm worth and have more fee earning downtime than be constantly busy with fee earning clients but feel slightly 'cheated'.

To put this scenario into perspective, I do have marketing and PR skills which can command a higher hourly rate, which my VA friend does not, but it just shows that limiting yourself to a certain geographical area may put a ceiling on the price you can charge. This friend actually started out charging £15 per hour but was bartered down to £12.50 per hour in her early days as a VA by a client and now cannot seem to remove herself from this price bracket, as people will recommend her and of course they tell their contacts how much they pay for her help.

At the other end of the scale, I know a VA who charges £30 an hour so that he attracts a certain kind of clientele. His hourly rate is set high on purpose to remove the chance of requests from start up businesses and people that cannot afford him and this allows him to concentrate on delivering a premium service to a smaller client base.

I have experimented with different hourly rates over the past few years, starting originally at £25 but as I didn't have the confidence as a self employed VA at the start to back this up, I allowed myself to be bargained down by a client in my early days to £23 per hour and then again to £20 per hour where I found my comfort zone for a while.

When you set a high hourly rate you also set certain expectations and without a track record of happy clients to justify what I was charging, I became uncomfortable asking for £25 per hour. This was why I took the decision to charge £20 per hour to all my clients (as I didn't like the thought that people may talk and wonder why they were being charged different rates!) and at this level of hourly rate I started to bring in a good stream of clients to work with.

Pricing myself too high initially made it less likely that I would take on a new client and sometimes it's better to be realistic and get the work in than not be working at all! Once I had started to establish trust with my clients and had some positive testimonials for my work, I could gradually start to increase my hourly rate. Once your clients know that you are good and they trust you, often they would rather absorb the extra pound an hour or whatever you decide to charge rather than lose you and have to start over with another VA. I know in my own life that when my cleaner announced that her prices were going up by 50p an hour in 2006, I just carried on paying. Then again she raised her price again by 50p an hour in 2007 and I didn't want the hassle of going elsewhere plus I trust her with keys to my house and to be in the house when I'm not there so I'd rather just pay the extra money rather than have to find someone else, establish trust and educate them as to my preferences. It's the same when you are a VA.

INCREASING YOUR RATES

If you do put up your rates whilst you are working with a client, you may find that not all clients will be as philosophical as this and may find the price increase too much for their business to stand and leave, so again, be mindful of your target market. In my case, when I raised my prices from £20 per hour to £25 per hour understandably I did lose a couple of clients because they felt my new price was too much but these were clients that I could afford to lose – I hadn't had much regular work from them and it became more hassle than it was worth to keep ringing them to see how I could help. With the clients who <u>were</u> using my services the price increase didn't affect their willingness to continue using me as I had already demonstrated my worth on the tasks I had fulfilled to date, and as they had successful, growing businesses themselves, they recognised the need for ongoing, capable, proactive support.

Going forward, when a new client asks me now what my hourly rate is and I reply £25 per hour plus VAT, some are put off by how high it is and some don't bat an eyelid. The ones who are happy to pay me what I ask for are the ones I want – they are generally more successful in their own business so they will have regular, ongoing work to give me, they appreciate that I am becoming 'part of their team' and once they start to rely on my help, the thought of getting a new VA and training them up in something that I can do perfectly well will be more hassle than trying to save a few pounds.

I tend to have the view that if a client thinks that my hourly fee is too much for them, they are very welcome to find another VA to assist – there are hundreds of VAs out there who charge £15 per hour and if they do find a good VA who they can use who will charge them this rate then there are no hard feelings. Every business person has to manage their finances, so it's understandable that they will want the best deal for themselves. But for you as the VA, this is where it is so important to establish a niche – it helps you command the rate that you want.

DEMONSTRATE VALUE, NOT COST

If I'm speaking to someone who is a prospective client, my 'marketing head' naturally comes on when I am talking to them about the tasks they want completed. I often make suggestions of how a task could be approached, which gives them a bit of 'free advice' but it also showcases my expertise on this subject. If writing something in the right way or in a way that would be more profitable for them is important, then the client might decide that they want my help with the work, regardless of the hourly cost. They see the value of having me assist them, which is why I can confidently state my rate of £25 per hour plus VAT. They either pay it or leave it. A lot pay it, and a lot leave it! But I have had enough clients who pay it to know that it is a fair price for my services and these clients continue to be happy with the service. However these clients are the ones who want and value my marketing niche. If all they wanted was data inputting or some envelopes stuffing, then it would be madness for them to pay £25 per hour for that (however I have had one or two clients who have asked for exactly this and I've completed the work happily – as long as I get the hourly rate I charge, it would also be madness for me as a business person to turn it away!)

A great idea that some VAs do (and I've seen other kinds of businesses like Life Coaches also do this), is to have 3 different levels of support – a kind of 'Bronze, Silver and Gold' pricing structure. This is a way to have different levels of pricing to basically have some kind of support for everyone, allowing those who need the help but who are put off by a higher rate, access some assistance at a price that they can afford. I never adopted this pricing strategy because within my business offer I do have a service that clients can access which starts from a rate of £25 per month so this is very cost effective! It is a Virtual Receptionist service so they can have their incoming calls answered by a professional Receptionist and it gives a great first impression of their business whilst ensuring that their callers don't hang up – which many would do if confronted by an answering machine! This way, if a possible client does like the idea of working with me, they can choose to use this service to access some kind of help in their business which not only frees up their time but also creates a great image of their business, and at the rate I charge for this, they can access this help very easily. This gives my business something to suit every small businesses budget.

PRICING TECHNIQUE

When you are looking at what price to charge for your work as a Virtual Assistant it's not enough to simply pick a number out of thin air as long as it is in line with the average VA rate. You need to be certain that the rate you choose will make you money because there is no point in selling your services at that rate if you are losing money by doing so. In addition, you need to ensure that your business is viable. If you cannot set an hourly rate that pays you what you need to earn without pricing yourself out of the typical VA market, then it's likely that you will not secure enough clients at that rate to make your business work and you'd probably be better off doing something else.

There is a technique to coming up with your hourly rate and whilst the formula is the same, the outcomes will be as unique as the individuals doing the sums, because every business is different. I learned this technique on a course that I went on when I started my business. It was a free course run by my local Business Link, which showed me how to start marketing my business and how to price my service and I'd encourage everyone setting up in business to go to their local Business Link to see what courses they can access too. The pricing segment of this course was very useful to me at the time because I did have an idea of what I'd like to charge but I wasn't sure if I'd make a profit at that rate so the formula helped me to calculate my 'break-even' point, meaning that I could ensure that I'd make a profit.

Every business will have different overheads and every business will therefore have a different 'break-even' point, so it's not wise just to set your price to be the same as your competitor. To calculate the right rate for you, do an in depth analysis of what you need to earn to survive, divide it by the number of hours you plan to work to achieve this, add on a 20% margin for profit and see what figure you arrive at.

For example when I first started out I needed to earn £1000 per month minimum to cover my part of the household bills, and I needed £250 a month to run my business with the various networking memberships I was paying into plus my phoneline rental and stationery etc. I needed to earn **at least** £1250 per month and I wanted to work for 4 hours a day to achieve this so I could spend the 'other' working 4 hours a day to complete marketing activities to bring the business in.

If I took what I needed to survive (£1250 pm) and divided it by the number of fee earning hours I wanted to work (4 a day, 5 days a week) then my hourly figure based upon a 4.5 week month is £13.88. Add a 20% profit margin and my hourly rate becomes £16.66. This means that at a £20 per hour VA rate I'm doing well but I cannot charge £15 an hour like some other VAs can because then I'd be working at a loss.

This is a very simplistic overview and the 'starting in business' courses that you can access for free locally will be much more in depth and will help you consider your individual circumstances. They will show you everything that needs considering, such as cost of marketing your business, depreciation on equipment purchased, cost of business premises (if you take these on), cost of stationery and other variables. As it is important to get up to date business advice when you are starting out, I'd always recommend getting this kind of specific advice from a business advisor. In addition, the free courses that you can go on are a great place to do some initial business networking, as there will be others on the course with you who are also starting out and it's a good chance to practice your business communication skills!

Once you have followed the business advisor's plan and arrived at an hourly rate, (including a margin for profit), if it is about the same as the 'average' VA hourly fee – you can safely charge the rate you want to or a little more, knowing that you won't be losing money. One thing to bear in mind however, is that you will work out your hourly rate depending on the hours you *expect* or *want* to work. This will differ from person to person. Some VAs will want to work a 40 hour week like in an employed job and some will want to be 'part time'. To achieve the income that you want you actually need to have billable work to do for all those hours to meet your targets. This means that you won't be working at full billing capacity straightaway. At the start you may be doing more marketing for new business than fee earning activity, but when you build your steady client base up the balance of the work you do will change and you'll more likely be charging out more hours than looking for work! It all takes time but you'll get there in the end with determination and adaptability.

Getting the initial price right can be a daunting task but once you hit upon a price you are happy with, you can forget about it and concentrate your efforts on bringing in the work. With no work to do you will earn nothing, so spend some time on setting your price but don't let it distract you from the real work of getting clients on board.

BILLING SYSTEM

Experience and often trial and error are the keys to your ongoing success so don't be afraid to try new things. One of the ways in which I have taken on board this advice within my own business and eliminated 'bad debt' was to innovate a new billing system, and this strategy if you choose to adopt it, will help you make money, work with clients proactively and eliminate 'down time' which are pockets of non-chargeable client chasing time!

When I started my business, I set my hourly rate and kept a timesheet of clients' work completed so I knew exactly what to charge each client. At the end of the month I would work out the client's bill from this and issue their invoice which I stated on the invoice should be paid within 14 days of receipt. This didn't always work out. It is an 'old fashioned' system and leaves you as the supplier vulnerable to non-payment. I would find that clients would sing my praises when I helped them to get out of a certain situation, or clean up their paperwork, but when the billing time came, the relief they felt at the time I assisted them was gone, and they had no motivation to pay my invoice. I would have to spend time chasing several clients asking when the bill would be paid, which I disliked doing but I wasn't going to work for free!

I heard about another 'service based' business in my area who charged their time in 'bundles' which was paid by the client up front and decided to adopt this strategy for my own business. I can liken it to a 'pay as you go' mobile phone voucher, in that you pay 'up front' for the hours you use and 'top up' that balance if the hours left are running low. I decided that I would sell my time in ten hour 'Time Bundles' so if a client wanted to work with me I would issue an invoice for £250 plus VAT to be paid immediately (or before work would start). Then any time worked would be logged on the timesheet as before but rather than time being logged as 'to be charged' – time accumulating - my method meant that available time would be reduced. When we got to a stage where I had completed 9 hours work I would inform the client of the status and ask them if they would like me to issue another time bundle invoice?

By simply turning the 'traditional' invoicing system on its head I eliminated bad debt – if the client didn't pay the invoice up front then I didn't do the work! I would ensure a positive cash flow within my business which meant that I could in turn, pay my own suppliers on time, which then gets you a good reputation for payment and suppliers are more likely to accommodate you when they know they can rely on you to settle your bills!

Another benefit of this system that I didn't anticipate at the start was that it cancelled non productive 'down time'. I no longer had to spend time chasing clients for non-payment (which is time that you cannot charge for!) and I no longer had to do weekly or fortnightly 'ring rounds' to ask clients if they needed any help. They would come to me! Once the client has paid up front they understandably want you to get to work for them straightaway and they want to get their moneys' worth. They will approach you with tasks to do and so you'll be able to spend all of your time on either fee earning jobs, on business marketing (which you'll always need to do an element of to keep work rolling in) and on your own business admin, but never have to waste time doing activities like ring rounds that don't always yield results! The Time Bundle really is a win-win concept!

I even started to expand the possibilities of the Time Bundle at one stage and promoted to new clients that if they wanted to save money they could purchase a 'Double Bundle' which was a 20 hour time bundle (charged at £500 plus VAT) and if they opted for this then I would actually give them 21 hours of work, so they got one hour free. It was worth it to me to give one hour free in return for a larger upfront payment. This is another variation on the technique which some service industries use which is 'get a 10% reduction on your bill if you pay before a certain date'. I did have one client who used to buy 'Double Bundles' from me, but the majority of my clients had more of a tighter cash flow themselves, so they only wanted to opt for one Time Bundle at a time. Whatever number of hours you choose to package your time into, the 'pay up front' concept is a great one for your ongoing business stability.

MAKING MONEY IN YOUR SLEEP

This is something that (understandably!) appeals to a lot of people. Setting up passive income streams from your business is something that you can develop, but it does take a lot of time and effort to get it working. I'll briefly outline all the ways I have come across to create passive income so you can try or reject as you see fit.

One idea I heard several years ago was that it is possible to set up a phone number with a recording facility at the other end, have clients dictate their documents or letters into this phone number then get an overseas VA to type it up – all of this would be done literally while you were sleeping! However, in practice I've never heard a VA's experience of doing this. I imagine it would be a delicate balancing act – 'distance managing' an overseas VA with your clients' work, then I would want to copy check it as I wouldn't want anything going out to a client that I hadn't checked or approved.

OUTSOURCING

When I first started out as a VA, I did a course where the idea of having 'VA Associates' was promoted as a great way to achieve passive income. The idea was that you would outsource some of your work to another VA (perhaps if you had more on than you could handle) and you'd charge out their time under your hourly rate and pay them a lower rate. In principle I can see that this kind of arrangement makes sense, however I have gone down this route a couple of times and found that it ended up being more hassle than it's worth in practise. Firstly, you have to find a VA who is willing to do your clients work at a lesser rate than you charge yourself because your client will certainly not pay any extra for work they have asked you to do. So if you charge your time at £20 an hour, you need to find a VA who charges £15. Then, you need to fully brief this VA on what the clients' preferences are and how they like things done. If you decided to use this VA regularly then you would have to view this initial extra time spent as the upfront cost of developing this arrangement and at least once you get into a routine with the VA you won't have to do this again! Then the work will actually be completed and returned to you. At this stage, personally I would check the work, because the client has entrusted this job to me, therefore the buck stops at my door. It is my reputation that would be affected if the client decided that the work wasn't up to standard, so I would definitely make sure that it was. If there is anything that is unclear then I would have to go back to the VA and clarify so that I am fully up to speed in case the client queries the work or aspects of it. After this I'd present the work to the client and charge them as normal, paying the VA for their part in the work.

The trouble with this for me is that I found by the time I'd done all of this I could have just done the job myself quicker! Maybe it's because of the kind of clients I had at the time. My clients are entrepreneurs generally, so they have lots of ideas, lots of projects on the go, use lots of different systems and internet resources, so knowing all the URL's and login details firstly takes a little time to pass on, then describing the way around each website and how to do things all takes more time. If I had been assigned a simple typing project by a client and needed to pass on something very straightforward like this to another VA then this arrangement may have worked better in my case.

I did delegate some 'Associate' work to a fantastic lady who was very fast and paid as much attention to detail as I did. We'd met at a business networking meeting and she had expressed an interest in helping me with some of my client work. We negotiated a rate that I would pay her whilst charging the time out higher to the client and I have no complaints whatsoever with this lady's quality of work. However even when I had a fantastic VA to outsource to, who was on the same wavelength as me, it still ended up being hassle for me as I always had to check everything before passing it to the client. Not because I didn't trust her, but because I felt it was my job to have the answer to whatever the client may ask about the work.

Of course you can only charge the client for time spent completing the work, not the time you spend briefing another VA and then checking the work, as it's not the client's issue that you have outsourced. As far as they are concerned they have given the work to you and you will do it, so by using an Associate, I was creating extra pockets of time in my day that I could not charge for. To me that didn't make sense. Maybe I was being too controlling and should have relaxed a bit more about meticulously checking everything, but when you run a small business your reputation is everything. You spend a great deal of time in building up a positive image, nurturing your clients so that they give you testimonials that you can use to get new clients through the door and delivering on your word, so that your business stands for something. I didn't find it easy to be casual about that and so outsourcing didn't work in my case. But that's not to say that it won't work for you. The trick is to find the level of risk that you are comfortable with and use that as your boundary.

EMPLOYING OTHER PEOPLE

A few years into my business, I had more work than I could possibly handle alone and as I had invested in renovating my outbuilding at home to become an office for the business, I had a place that I could call 'work' and therefore someone else could too! I took the step of employing an assistant to work with me in the business, generally running the day to day office such as telephone answering, opening the post, ordering stationery, making teas and coffees and speaking to clients. This assistant was a lovely girl who I found through placing an advert and my plan was to train her up to reach a level where she could take on some of my VA admin work for clients, so that I could charge her time out at my rate, but of course she was paid a fixed salary.

This arrangement worked better for me than using an Associate VA because as my employee I felt more in control of her work and clients would also get to know her personally so it would be easier to manage the business all round. As opposed to an Associate VA who you would never introduce to your clients in case they decided that if the Associate was being paid £5 less for the same work then they might 'cut out the middleman' and go to the Associate direct!

There were many upsides to having an employee in terms of being able to grow the business but a downside was that they were salaried so they needed paying whether they did the work for you or not. As the principle VA in your business it would be up to you to bring in the work that your staff could physically 'do' but your staff wouldn't bring in new business – at least not at first. In addition, the legislation surrounding employment means that you have to be very careful to not inadvertently fall foul of the law, as it could end up costing you dearly. Not wanting to go through the hassles of employment is one of the reasons that many small business owners cite as their motivation for using a Virtual Assistant in the first place, and whilst there is nothing to stop you from growing your business using the employment model, you will need to ensure that you take good advice to stay legally compliant if you do.

In my case, my assistant left the business after a few months for personal reasons and I decided at that time not to replace her because it didn't suit my impending life circumstances to have to find, train up and settle in a new employee. I was newly pregnant and therefore would be planning a 'maternity leave' in the near future.

INFORMATION PRODUCTS

Another way to generate passive income from your business is to package up your knowledge as an 'information product' (like via writing books, giving tele-seminars and selling audio products) and sell it. This is a way of 'doing the work once' and being paid for it over and over. Of course to get to the 'income rolling in' stage you have a lot of work to do in terms of creating the original product and initially promoting it, but this is another avenue open to you.

MEMBERSHIP CLUB

A residual income can also be generated through the creation of a membership based 'club' or website where clients would pay you for a subscription to be a part of it. However to attract clients for this kind of venture in the first place you would need to spend time developing an attractive offer and continually update it to ensure that members stayed, so this is a little more 'active' than 'passive' but it's another thing to consider. So as you can see 'passive income' may be many things but it does require some action!

OTHER SERVICES

A great way I have found to boost my business income has been to offer my Virtual Receptionist service to clients which puts a Receptionist onto their phone line so they don't lose business through missed calls. This is a valuable service to clients in their business which also provides me with a steady monthly income and the more clients you have signed up to it, the more you earn! I have found this a useful way to bring in clients to my business whom I can then 'upsell' my other services to and they are more likely to listen to how I can help them as they are already a client! This service is a 'bolt on' to my core business activity and any Virtual Assistants looking to use this service in their own business can find more information at *www.thedreampa.co.uk/services.html*

FUNDING

Before we move on to actually getting your first client and launching your business, the last thing to consider in a chapter about money is funding. The different available funding pots are changing all the time and when one funding stream runs out it may not be replaced, so you will need to take individual advice on whether you are eligible for any of the existing business funding. There are different criteria for start up businesses and for more established businesses, and your local Business Link would be a good place to seek individual help to see whether you can get this kind of cash injection to your business at the start. Good luck!

Getting Your First Client - You've Launched!

Now we are getting to the exciting part! Taking on your first client is a big step and when you have done it, do take a moment to pat yourself on the back! But only a moment – the real work starts then! This is a landmark stage in your business, as this is the time when all your planning pays off and your business goes from 'pre start' to actually trading. Your 'trading from' date will usually be the date upon which you issue your first invoice so if you are planning to use Time Bundles as I do, the first client stage marks your business start date. Well done! You've launched!

In my experience, Virtual Assistants have a few things in common. They know that they are excellent at the work they are being paid by the client to do, but often, as this is the first time the VA has run a business before, setting the terms under which they wish to do business can be a bit scary. They are not sure what to say or how to approach 'formalising' the arrangement and many VAs have asked me what to put in their contract.

Personally, I no longer use a contract (I did very briefly at the start as mentioned in a previous chapter) but I am asking clients for payment up front and won't do the work until I get it, plus I have a business 'Terms & Conditions' statement to give to them, so I don't feel the need to do more than that. By all means, have a contract if you think it is the best way to proceed for you – maybe you will feel more confident in your dealings with clients if the terms are agreed right from the start. However, as a VA you are certain to be a naturally gifted communicator, with the ability to relate to people at differing levels, so I would trust yourself to be able to negotiate terms with clients as you go. This will give you more flexibility than tying you into a set agreement from the start.

Having a contract in many cases is a confidence issue and once you get started and experience working with clients directly, you will see that they are just human beings, like you. Decide what you are prepared to accommodate within your business and state it in your Ts & Cs, giving this to any new clients along with your 'upfront' invoice. This 'Terms & Conditions' statement is something that covers your preferences whilst acknowledging the client's possible wishes. It is not a compulsory legal requirement, but a wise suggestion allowing you to have clear definitions of working practices and boundaries at the start so that misunderstanding does not get chance to set in to your relationships with your clients. If everyone knows and agrees to the terms of business at the outset then there is less opportunity for disagreement later on and your Ts & Cs will also show your prospective clients that you have thought about and considered potential pitfalls to virtual working and have created a solution to these problems thereby showcasing your problem solving skills. For example; one of my terms is my hours of work. I have put that I work between 9am to

5pm Monday to Friday. However I recognise that some clients may, on occasion, need assistance outside of these hours, so I have stated in my Ts & Cs that I can try to accommodate them outside of these hours if we agree something in advance. I am happy to assist 'out of hours' when I can, as long as my schedule is open, but I don't want the client to *expect* to be able to reach me and gain an immediate response after my preferred working hours.

PRACTICALITIES

Once you have given your client a contract or a Terms & Conditions statement, and the expectations of either party have been addressed, you can get down to the work of 'doing the do'! When working virtually with a client in practice, they will often brief me on what they want (either by phone, in person or by email) then I will get on with their work from my home office. I work on one client's work at a time and I ensure that I give that work my 100% concentration, both to get it done quickly and accurately, and so the client gets their money's worth!

As a Virtual Assistant, you have to be aware of business on two fronts. Firstly, you will devote your focused attention to the clients' work and doing that well, but you also have to be mindful that whilst you are 'unavailable' to speak to anyone else (potential new clients for example), that your business appears to be available. When you worked for an employer you could just focus on the work they asked you to do and that's it, but as a self employed VA you also want to keep enquiries coming in from potential new clients, so that you have other clients to assist when the immediate work you are doing is over.

How you do this when you are working on another client is to ensure that your business is still 'open for business' and the best way to achieve this is to get a Virtual Receptionist[8]. This means that you can divert your office phone-line to the Virtual Receptionist to answer calls when you are unavailable, so whilst you have your brain engaged in another clients' book-keeping or mail-shot your callers are able to speak to your business to request a call back for help and advice on your services. Virtual Assistants often offer telephone answering/call minding services to their clients as a service within their business, so have to be especially careful to 'walk the talk' and use these services themselves. It doesn't create the right impression for a potential client to call a possible Virtual Assistant and reach his or her answer-phone!

I will always ensure that my business phone and mobile phone are both diverted to my Receptionist before I start on a clients' tasks. Then, I do the job in hand and when it's as far as it can be at that time, I will 'log off' the client's work, complete my timesheet and either send the completed work back to the client or give them an update, but I will also schedule the next slot when I will work on that project or with that client. This way there is always enough time blocked out of my diary to complete the tasks I have to do and

I can easily see where I have room to make new appointments or attend networking meetings.

MANAGE YOURSELF

When you are working on a clients' task they are counting on you to have the razor sharp focus that they themselves may sometimes lack, which means you have to manage your own working environment to minimise your distractions. It's a good idea to set yourself routines such as only checking and responding to email twice a day and turning it off at all other times so you are not distracted by the new mail icon appearing at the bottom of your screen. By having your phone diverted, you are creating space in which to work uninterrupted and you can be more efficient with your own time by returning all your calls in one go once the clients' work is complete.

Remember, when you get some momentum in your business and have half a dozen clients on the go, they will all expect the same focused attention and immediate recall on the status of their workloads at an instant when they call you. If you don't have water-tight admin systems in place for you to manage your own work-load, it is easy to become unstuck! So get this framework in place for yourself from the start to help you scale your business up and down as your client base grows in the future.

'EXTRAS'

During the last two years I have been approached for advice from other VAs who have asked me things like how much I charge (answer: £25 per hour) and how do I bill for 'extras' such as postage and mileage (answer: I buy items at the time they are needed and itemise them separately on the next Time Bundle invoice so the client will pay for time in advance with the next bill but for consumables in arrears. I charge mileage at 40p/mile and review this figure annually).

Virtual Assistants have also asked me how they should do certain tasks such as accepting deliveries for other companies, because a client has requested it and they are unsure of the 'protocol' involved when clients make unfamiliar requests. My advice is only do what you are comfortable with – it's ok to say "No" to a client if you don't want to fulfil the kind of work they are asking for. They may of course choose to go somewhere else, but if you take on tasks that you don't want to do it's easy to feel resentful, and this isn't a productive emotion when you are running your own business!

In my case, I would not allow my business address to be used as a delivery address for someone else, because I am not operating from a commercial business park or high street premises. I have had a request for this a few times and have suggested the client uses a proper 'mail forwarding' address which I can supply, but I won't have their mail come to my own address. If a client working from home does not wish to inform his/her own clients about their postal address, then they can easily rent a PO Box address or use a serviced city centre office address to accept their incoming mail. These services do charge a fee - but they exist. You might also do as I have done and find a company whom you can refer clients to so they can have this service through you. It makes the clients' life a bit easier as they don't have to go elsewhere to find the aspect of help they need and you can just sort it out for them (ensuring the client knows this is an additional service and pays you for it separately!)

Several years ago a start up VA approached me for some advice because she was also asked about using her address for mail forwarding by a prospective client and she didn't want to sound unhelpful by saying an outright "No", or unprofessional by saying that she didn't know if she'd want to offer this kind of service. What she did was to agree to allow her address to be used then she came to me to ask how to do it! I had to say that I don't actually do this, but advised finding a mail forwarding address that she could use.

It highlighted to me that there is no 'set' model of how to operate as a VA. Some VAs will happily carry out some services, some won't – it's individual. If you want some breathing space to think about a clients' enquiry though, it's a good tip to say "I've never been asked that before, let me research the implications of this and get back to you", which allows you time to think about it and decide your stance on the issue. I would always advise VAs to only do the tasks and services that they are happy and comfortable doing and stick to that. There are no 'rules' as such and you don't want to end up stuck in a situation that was not of your choosing through being too nice to say "No"!

WORD OF MOUTH

Over time you will get to know your clients very well and their repeat business and positive word of mouth will be invaluable to you as a small business owner. Every business needs a good turnover of new clients or enough business from existing clients to keep going, and the only way to get either of these is to do your job well and to look after your clients so that they remain loyal to you. This kind of relationship cultivation takes time and effort but will be worth it in the end as you begin to develop a positive track record.

A lot of Virtual Assistants actually secured their first client from their existing contact circles - it was a person already known to them, perhaps a friend of a friend or even their spouse who needed assistance in business! This is a good way to get the ball rolling on your VA activities, so look at your immediate network of friends, family and business people you know to see who is around that may need help and see if you can agree to support them. Even if you have to do a few 'skinny' jobs at less than your preferred hourly rate at the start, just to get moving, it will be worth it in the long term, as long as you do raise your hourly fee to its 'usual' level soon after!

A good way to offer an early customer a lower rate without jeopardising your ongoing 'full' rate is to say that as a business launch discount you are offering the first 3 clients a rate of £x or a special deal of one hour's work free for every 2 hours paid (or similar). The point is not to do yourself out of profit, but to just get the ball rolling. Just be sure to revert to your preferred hourly rate as soon as you can for new clients after a certain point.

I got my own first client through business networking. I was still working at my employed job at first so it was a real juggling act, working for my employer during the day and doing my 'own' work once I got home. I remember having to use my annual leave from work to participate in networking events for my business and felt guilty at the time that I couldn't tell my employer my intentions, as I've always preferred to be upfront and honest with people. This largely prompted my decision to resign from my day job and concentrate on my business before I had enough clients to make the business viable.

I leapt from the 'security' of employment with only 2 clients on board which was not nearly enough to survive, but I had decided that it was a 'now or never' moment. I either had to jump and see if I could fly or stay in the nest of employment, wondering "what if". Staying was not an option for me so I leapt and it's the best thing I ever did. It has been hard financially at times, but things improve with consistent effort and the confidence I gained from being in control of my own future is priceless. Through working for myself I have learned sales skills, developed my creativity, become comfortable as a public speaker and more unflappable in general. I love being able to take my child to school each day without having to use the school breakfast club and being able to finish work mid afternoon if I feel like it on a Friday 'just because' is great. I often sit in the local family oriented pub at 5pm on a Friday with a drink, my children and my husband, waiting for our bar meal and think that if I was still at my last job I'd be hard at it in the office right now and wouldn't be getting home for another hour! The freedom gained from making that leap is worth trading in all the company cars and pension schemes I had in my previous role.

So if you don't have anyone in your immediate circle who needs VA assistance, the best way to get your first client is to go to local networking events like I did. Many take place on an evening so if you are still working you can find one to attend; your local Chamber of Commerce or Business Link will be able to advise you of what's in your area. There are also plenty of breakfast groups and lunchtime events so whatever your working pattern you can find something to suit.

Once you get out there and start talking to people, you will often hear about other networking events locally to try out as a potential place to find new clients, and your business contact network will grow. Bringing in the first few clients to your business is a real learning curve but practice makes perfect and need to feel like they can rely on a VA and if they always get your answering machine they won't be as confident that their message will be delivered to you as they would if they had spoken to a human being - we all like the reassurance of the personal touch.

If you are struggling to keep on top of your books because you are busy fulfilling your clients' work, then hire a book-keeper to assist you. If you are finding it hard to update your own business website, then find a web developer who can help you. You don't have to and maybe shouldn't, do everything yourself! As you will probably tell your clients, it makes sense for you to concentrate on what you are good at and let someone else more capable attend to the tasks you could do yourself but don't need to, so get the support you need.

Another secret to success is to let your clients feel like they are your only client when you are dealing with them. Remember their birthday, ask about their holiday, remember their best clients' name! All of this sounds like common sense but it can be tricky when you get to a stage where you have many clients to remember the personal details of them all. However, this kind of attention to detail helps the relationship to develop and promotes trust. As VAs we are probably best placed to actually achieve this aim through our excellent organisational skills in any case, so make notes on your client files about these 'personal talking points' and refer to your notes during conversations. Your clients will love that you have taken an interest in their lives and will be

the more experience you get the easier it will become in the future. Succeeding at these early steps also gives you a big confidence boost in your business, both affirming that you are on the right track personally and also cementing the skills and phrases that you will use in the future to find new clients. You quickly learn what prospective clients what to know about when encountering a Virtual Assistant for the first time, so you can say more of the things they want to hear - making you faster at converting them from enquirers into paying clients!

The next chapter will focus on how to manage your clients and keeping business ticking over...

You're On The Road
- Now What?

Once you have secured your early clients and are fulfilling their work, your thoughts will turn to sustaining your client base and juggling all these individuals effectively. Now you have to negotiate the balancing act which is serving all your existing clients with continuing to manage your own business work and continual marketing for new business to keep work steady when you have a natural turnaround of clients on your books. Plus, you will want to have some life of your own too!

Here is where the importance of starting with the end in mind really comes in. If you decided at the beginning, before you had taken on any clients at all, what kind of working pattern you would like, how much time you would spend on client work and where you would set the boundaries to enjoy your own free time, you will be better placed to manage your business now.

BE ADAPTABLE

The realities of dealing with actual paying clients can make you look at your business differently. You may find that marketing for new work takes up more time than you had originally anticipated or that the kind of work you thought you would enjoy, you actually don't. So don't be afraid to tweak your initial ideas once you

have the experience to educate your c However having some mental framework of v originally wanted is really helpful in focus efforts towards achieving those goals in the lo and keep you going down the right path.

YOUR VALUES

You can always change and adapt the activit business does as you go along, but there ar qualities that you should adhere to withi business which are fundamentals. Whatever yo order to be successful, it is advised to add demonstrate these qualities. The main one I be to be credible. Become known for doing what you will do. Be consistent with your messag opinions and always deliver. Your reputation i will attract or repel potential clients so ensuri it is positive is essential. If you have promised something, ensure you do it. If you are too bu the help you need. Don't be afraid to outsource yourself when you need assistance – one person do everything all the time – and by this I necessarily mean taking on an Associate, just you have a task within the running of your business that someone else can do better, delegate it to them.

When you 'walk your talk', you will become son who is trusted, and trust brings business. If yo missing calls as you are not available to answer phone, then get a telephone answering service. P

more likely to tell others how great you are as a result. Which equates to more business for you!

THE DOWNSIDE?

There is however a potential down-side to being fantastic(!) which is a universal VA problem. This is the fact that when one of your clients needs you, maybe if they are having an emergency, they will often not consider that you may be busy with another client, and may expect you to drop everything to assist them! This is both a compliment because they obviously see that you are the person to help them and they trust you, however it can also be a delicate arrangement, because you have to carefully appease their concerns whilst ensuring that you continue to give your other clients the attention they are used to.

If an emergency comes up and you had plans for another clients' work at that time and you can easily re-schedule the other client then you will be ok, but if you can't then you'll need your diplomatic skills to communicate to the client with the emergency exactly when you can help. It's never nice to have to let a client down, but when you are busy and have your own successful business you will have to manage the expectations of many clients and this places demands on the available time that you will have.

As my business started to become successful and I took on clients and achieved media coverage for the business, something that I would encounter a lot of was people who wanted to become VAs themselves, approaching me for advice. This was why I decided to write this book as I wanted to help everyone who asked but I also have a very busy business of my own to run, with clients who all expected my full attention, not to mention my family who I had started the business to see more of! After helping as many people as I could by pointing them towards resources like VA websites and offering my own experiences as examples for them to learn from, I found that similar questions were being asked of many people and I was repeating myself a lot in answering them. After thinking a bit about how I could solve this problem I used the themes from the questions people asked me to create a framework for this book, and over time, I started to write a little each day to eventually finish the work you hold in your hands!

Having created this resource, I have now effectively protected my own time, because any Virtual Assistants who want to learn more can read this book. My time is now freed up for existing clients and for other business building activities such as creating and running the Virtual Assistant courses which I did recently. The lesson here is that once your VA business gets going, you'll find unexpected requests made of you, either by clients or other people, and the trick is to find a way to fulfil these requests (if you want to of course!) whilst still keeping everything else moving!

ASK FOR FEEDBACK

Perhaps one of the most important secrets to success as a Virtual Assistant when you are in the throes of running your own business, is to not be afraid of asking for feedback – good and bad. In order to give your clients the kind of service they need and therefore encourage them to be your best advertising message through positive word of mouth, you need to check that they are satisfied with the service they are getting and ask if there is anything else that you could do that would be useful to them.

If they have a negative comment about an aspect of your service, welcome it. It's not a criticism of you, it's simply them saying how what you do could be even better and they need to feel comfortable in telling you these things. They may have a valid point in which case you could address it and then they and your other clients will be happy, or it could be a point which you cannot directly fix but you could do something else to make it right. It can be hard to hear negative things when you think you are doing a great job but its better that they tell you so you can fix it rather than your clients telling everyone else but you, so you are wondering why you have few clients with no idea of how to increase them.

I carry out regular feedback surveys within my business to ensure that the lines of communication are kept open between my clients and myself and also to ensure they know that they can come to me with any problems. The frequency of the surveys depends upon what services my clients take from the business, but the thing that they will always have in common is that I make the communications personal by targeting my writing. Even if I am sending out an email 'en masse' I will write it as if it is to just one person. This will give it a more friendly tone and make the reader feel more compelled to respond to my request for information if they feel that I am genuinely concerned about their views and keen to take on board suggestions so that my business can grow. The worst thing that you can do is to write something like:

"Hi everyone, I'm asking all my clients for feedback, will you let me have your views…"

It's just so impersonal and it's obvious that you have written it to a lot of people in one go. There is less motivation for them to respond to your request as they will be busy and as they see you have asked other people too, they may feel it doesn't matter if they don't respond. Then you get no feedback!

Something more personal will generally attract more responses. For example:

"Thank you for your custom and loyalty over the last 6 months and I am writing to ask you how you feel about the service I have delivered so that I am able to improve your experience over the next 6 months…"

The tone is warmer, it is more friendly in its approach and it is more likely to get a response. Try it and see for yourself. You may find that you get better results when you use certain words in your letters or when you seek feedback at certain times of year. You will get to know your clients very well and will be able to judge what methods achieve the most success over time so try different things and see. Just make sure that you act upon the feedback received, otherwise it was a waste of time in doing the survey.

TAKE CARE OF YOURSELF

When striving to achieve success in your business it is sometimes easy to work round the clock, put everyone else's needs before your own and to basically work yourself into the ground. Be aware of this pitfall and don't do it! There will be times when you *have* to work long days whilst you are building up a reputation but ultimately these should be balanced out with days of self care. You are the person your clients are relying on therefore you need to be operating in your peak state to deliver the kind of results you can be proud of. Get your rest, have time off for fun, get your nails done – whatever you need to feel 'human' again. There's no point in making money if you don't get to enjoy it. What good is being the richest person in the graveyard? Part of having a successful business is being able to enjoy the fruits of your labour, so don't feel you have to become a workhorse to be successful.

GOING FOR GROWTH?

Once you have got your business off the ground and running at a steady pace with a nice bunch of clients to serve, you may start to look at other ways you can expand your business offering. Either by taking on a member of staff and more clients, or by innovating and considering new ways to assist both your own clients and potential new 'pools' of clientele that you may wish to serve in the future.

If your plan is to run a business that will eventually support you when you choose not to work, you will need to look at the factors involved in creating employment, moving a 'bedroom business' to proper premises and the legalities that are involved with growing such as VAT and Health & Safety legislation. Creating a business plan is the best way to plot out your desired path on paper, to test the viability of it before you actually undertake the necessary steps and it will also help you to spot potential costly errors before they are made.

Businesses in general need to constantly move and grow to survive – businesses that remain exactly the same, year after year find that the world changes around them and they stagnate. In our industry Virtual Assistance is seen as 'cutting edge'. It is the latest way of working. It is a new working pattern that could eventually replace the traditional working model of an employee travelling in to a business premises, working for 8 hours a day then returning home. Either future employees could become a virtual workforce or companies will use self employed VAs to do the work. In an employed setting being 'virtual' has great benefits for both employer and employee with companies being able to cut costs on the heating and lighting on a business premises if all the staff are virtual, and the employee benefits by being able to work to suit their schedule therefore creating a better work life balance which in turn makes them happier and more productive.

As a Virtual Assistant you are already in an industry that is leading the way into the future, so it's great if you can build upon that momentum by continuing to innovate and look for new markets to serve. Business owners that you meet whilst out networking or at events will look to you as a leader, an innovator – purely because of the industry you have chosen.

I remember the realisation I had about a year or so into my business that not everyone was as 'up to speed' on working virtually and what it entails as I was. Of course, I didn't expect that everyone would know everything about how it works, but things that I considered 'basic' knowledge was actually far from it! I was using technologies like VoIP (Voice Over Internet Protocol) which is also known by the term 'Internet Telephony' (making phone calls over the internet). When I started the business in 2005 and quickly adopted this technology to help me run my business, I didn't realise that so many people at that time had no clue what it was. It is becoming more common now, but even as it becomes widespread, there is always a newer technology coming out to learn about. Blogs are a big thing now for businesses, both to market their business, interact with their customers and attract new clients. Hot on the heels of blogs are services that enable you to participate in 'microblogging', Twitter[20] being a great example of this.

The 'job title' of Virtual Assistant is a lot more commonplace now. People that I meet in business circles seem to know what it is, but there are still other people I meet that aren't sure (mainly some mums at the school gates and people I might meet in other personal circumstances such as nights out). However even just a few short years ago, a lot of business owners would say, "What's that then?" when I told them what I do for a living. A few would joke "does this mean you are a hologram?" and it was a good way to break the ice and tell them what I actually did. At least being a Virtual Assistant seems to peak other people's interest in a way that I think announcing that I'm an 'Accountant' wouldn't! (If my Accountant is reading this part of the book – no offence!)

LISTEN

When you are busy running your business and looking for areas in which to grow always listen to what your clients are saying. When you meet them or send them an email and ask, "How is business?" you should really listen to their replies as you could pick up ideas or patterns that will help you grow your own business. The people you are directly serving might just start to indicate a need for help in another area that you could fulfil or perhaps they may have noticed a pattern within their own clientele that could spark an idea.

One of my former clients was a bespoke tailor, ex Saville Row trained and absolutely impeccable in his appearance and his manner. He had re-located from London to

Yorkshire where he was looking to build up a client base of high net worth individuals who would want his made to measure suits - Saville Row quality but sold at 'Yorkshire' prices! His clients were Barristers, Premier League Footballers, High Growth Entrepreneurs and wealthy people who appreciated the cut and quality of one of his suits. His bespoke suits cost the client approximately £1500.00 each for a completely one off, tailored design. The client would have chosen his or her own fabric, lining, collar and had the garments fitted to their own body size and shape, created by hand and fit to the individual. This same suit made on Saville Row would have cost the client four times that amount, but my client had lower overheads being based from home and travelling to his clients, so that he could offer real value for money to this market.

When I worked with him, it was on a project to do promotional mailings to a cherry picked mailing list and follow this up with a phone call to the target client to see if they would agree to an appointment with the Tailor, so he could show them the quality of his fabrics and his work and potentially secure an order. I wouldn't normally have taken on a job like this because it involved 'cold calling' which is a task that I really dislike, but I had just employed my assistant at the time and she had a background in telemarketing and was happy to make the calls. Upon doing the ring-round to the various lawyers and entrepreneurs on the list and getting some initial feedback, a pattern that emerged was how busy these individuals were. These were people who in some cases, were employed, working long hours and with no time to fit in personal appointments like getting clothes dry cleaned or having suits fitted. It sparked an idea in me to consider offering a service aimed directly at high net worth individuals, to be a 'personal PA' – kind of like a concierge service, where I could do all the things that they hadn't time to do like take the dry cleaning and wait in for the gas man. Given that I had other clients to work for, running this kind of personal service would involve me employing lots of assistants who could do the running around for me – with me co-ordinating the venture, but I never really researched it fully enough as I'd just become pregnant so I had other more pressing matters to deal with first!

Until this idea came about I'd only ever done work for small business owners who I would meet whilst out networking for my business. Upon doing this ring-round job for the Tailor, it helped me to come up with this idea, so that's a great example of using your existing clients and what's going on around you as inspiration. It is not an idea that I'm planning to develop in the future now. The excitement I initially had for creating this kind of service has gone, and if I have learned one thing it is to always do what excites you and what you are passionate about. Being devoted to something will make it easier for you to ride out the tough times, so I'd never take on a project I was half hearted about. But always be on the look out for inspiration – what are the problems out there that need solving?

I heard recently about an American Virtual Assistance business that had packaged up their time to sell to clients in two ways. There was a 'Lite' package for people who just wanted a little help every day, a few calls making or keeping track of their diary for them for example. There was also a 'Dedicated' package aimed at clients who needed more full-time or in depth help such as research projects or data inputting. This VA firm promoted their services as, "an easy way for the client to access the help they want and clients can reach their Assistant by email, phone or fax – whichever they prefer!" Well, to be honest, this can be said of ALL VAs. We are all reachable by email, phone and fax and we can all do both short and longer term projects, so whilst the actual offer is nothing new, the way this firm marketed it is. By outlining which 'package' a potential client would need and steering them toward it, they made it easier for the client to see how they could be helped – a great example of innovation!

Maybe you can come up with a new way to do something and by having fresh ideas and continually striving to make your offer better than your competition, it is more likely that you'll still be in business and still enjoying it several years down the line!

To have a lasting, successful business it is important to get off to a good start. The next chapter highlights some of the common 'mistakes' that have been made by other Virtual Assistants when starting out, so you can steer clear of them and side-step any landmines!

The Mistakes That Most New VAs Make & How To Avoid Them...

In any start up business mistakes will be made - it's how we learn after all! In fact, one of my favourite sayings which I found on the bottom of one of those desk calendars with a 'quote of the day' on each page, says: "A mistake is evidence that someone has tried to do something". How true. It's better to get up and do something and make a mistake than to let fear of mistakes paralyse you from action. No-one ever did anything just by thinking about it so please don't ever be afraid to make a mistake in your business because it will stop you from growing if you do. However there are some common errors that I see repeated time and time again, which are worth being aware of so you don't make them when starting up your new VA business. It's best to learn from the ways of others to make the path right for you!

WRONG COMMUNICATION STYLE

Many Virtual Assistants become Virtual Assistants from a background as a PA, Secretary or Administrator and a lot come from large companies. Not all of course – the industry attracts people from many different backgrounds, but the thing we do all have in common is a talent for organisation, getting things done, often being someone's 'right hand'. Of course when someone from a 'big company' background starts up their own small business, the temptation is there to communicate with your potential clients as though you are still sat in a corporate office with other teams of support staff around you, because this is the only communication style that you know. I say DON'T DO IT!

Until someone points this out, a VA may not even realise they are communicating in this way, but speaking about your business and yourself as though you are the head of a large company is a major mistake. It can be a turn off for the very people you could be looking to attract as clients and if it doesn't turn them off, they may decide that you won't be interested in their 'little job' because you have so many other important things to do! The way a VA may inadvertently give this perception would be by communicating through their website or saying in person something like, "we always do it like this" or "we will do that", giving the impression that they have a staff of many when in fact they are a one person business.

This doesn't sound like a huge issue but to the end user – the client you are trying to attract - it either makes your business sound like something they can't afford or, it just won't 'speak' to them. The person you are standing in front of will hear 'vague' language like, "we will do this" whereas the more direct and powerful "I can help you by doing this, this and this" is a statement that makes people stand up and take notice! People like people who can take ownership of a task and if you are saying in no uncertain terms what exactly YOU will do, it is a more dynamic sales message than saying "we will sort it out by doing this" – who is "we" exactly? 'Owning' the job by communicating in a way that shows you are the person to solve their problem is the key to bringing in new business.

The only caveat to this point that I'll make is that it is fine to say, "we can help you like this…" if you really are a 'we'! If you do have a team of people to help you or if you do have at least one member of staff then saying 'we' is accurate, but I'd still recommend speaking to your prospects in the 'first person' as it's just so much more convincing.

If your concern is to try to make your business seem 'larger' than it is you can easily do this by having a receptionist take your calls (a virtual receptionist rather than a member of staff!) and having a prestigious office address to put on your business cards. This kind of service can be rented from plenty of suppliers and they will forward any incoming mail for you on to your home or another address you specify. If appearing bigger than a Sole Trader business will get you more clients then go for it! But don't automatically think that saying that you are a small business or a Sole Trader will put off potential clients, it won't! Especially if they are Sole Traders too!

People by nature tend to stick with what works, so if you find that communicating your business in a certain way seems to bring in the work then why change it? Just be aware when you are communicating your business that the language of marketing for a large company is very different to the language of marketing for a small one and it makes sense to put yourself in your customers' shoes after you have written some promotional communication, to see if the desired message has been communicated. Read what you have written back to yourself, as if you were that business owner you are trying to secure and see if it grabs you. Remember, most people will generally ask themselves the question, "what's in it for me?" when they are reading or hearing about something new, so be sure to address them. Tell them in no uncertain terms exactly what they will get from dealing with you and they will be more likely to use you!

BEING TOO GENERAL

The people you want to convince to become your clients are like all of us, bombarded daily with hundreds of advertising messages from TV, billboards, newspapers, conversations with people, trips to the supermarket, people with clipboards in the street and more! As human beings we have all had to learn to tune out to the 'non-essential' stuff in order to stay sane! Have you ever noticed how you can be completely unaware of something until something happens to force it into your consciousness, then you are aware of it everywhere? An example of this might be a car that you want to purchase. You know which one you want and in which colour and no-one else seems to have it, then you make the big purchase and drive the car away only to suddenly see loads of other people driving the same car in 'your' colour! It's because you have suddenly become aware of it, this car has entered your consciousness and now you are seeing it everywhere!

It is exactly the same with all humans. If we were acutely aware of everything going on around us then we'd never get anything done. We have the ability to filter out distant noises or become so accustomed to the way our own environment sounds that we don't notice it. Have you ever lived on a noisy street only to take a trip to the country and not be able to sleep because it's too quiet! Or vice versa – maybe people living somewhere more sparsely populated visiting central London for the night could be amazed at how people living here ever sleep because of the noise! This ability to immediately hear something, filter it and reject it in a split second is a massive bonus to humans to enable us to keep what bits of information we need and forget the rest, but for you, as a business person with a service to sell, it can make your job harder if you are not aware of it and adapt yourself accordingly.

By being quite generalist in the language you use to communicate what you do and by adopting an 'impersonal' tone with your website visitors, they won't be 'grabbed' by what they are reading. Their brain will filter the message, decide it's not for them and simply switch off. If, however, your message is specifically targeted to a certain audience and someone from within that audience is reading your website, they will think, "this firm is talking about me!" It will demonstrate to the reader that you understand their concerns and can address them and this is much more powerful in attracting customers than trying to sound vague, distant and 'corporate'.

TRYING TO SELL TO EVERYONE

One of the best books I ever read on sales skills and marketing said that generally nine out of ten people that you speak to will not be interested in your product or service. Sounds disappointing at first glance, doesn't it? But it is actually really freeing to realise that not everyone you speak to will be a customer. It takes the pressure off you from trying to 'sell' to everyone and to be honest, there is no greater turn off than someone giving you the 'hard sell'. It makes us back away from the 'seller' rather than be drawn to them! I've been to networking events where some people just don't 'get it'. They are like a dog with a bone when it comes to talking about their product or service – without actually establishing if I'm interested in hearing about it or in the market for it. They just launch into their tired old sales patter and leave me wondering how I can get away without seeming rude!

By realising that not everyone you meet will want your service you will be more humble when speaking to new people and will actually ask questions. You'll avoid the pushy 'hard sell' tactics which only serve to make you look desperate and you will be able to gently communicate what you do in a way that makes you the obvious choice for providing that service, if and when the business owner decides they need extra help. No-one is obliged to use you at all and whether they choose to use your service will very much depend on the impression you make. It's a well-known fact that 'people buy people' and by that I mean that people will be more likely to purchase from someone who they like. Pushy people are usually not liked very much, so please don't be one of them!

On the flip side, if nine out of ten people will not want your service – this means that one in ten will, and this is who you need to go after. This is where speaking directly and not in 'generalist' terms comes in when you are trying to attract new business. Identify the kinds of business that you either want to deal with, or that you know have a need for your services and aim your marketing towards them. If you have specialist knowledge of a certain industry then let people know it so you can become the choice for businesses in that industry. If you are speaking to a prospective customer in their language, then using terms that are specific to their industry or demonstrating a knowledge of their industry, will make them more likely to see you as someone who can assist, rather than the VA who says they can help 'anyone with anything'.

I made the mistake of being too vague when I was starting out, because technically, a VA *can* assist any business with any kind of support task. It felt like I'd be limiting my chances of getting new business by talking only to one or two particular sectors of the business community but in practice I found that the reverse is actually true. By being specific about who I could help, I got more clients that fitted the particular profile I was after. By telling people when I was out networking that I assisted Sole Traders and Partnerships, the radar was switched on for this kind of business. People who were Sole Traders pricked up their ears as I was talking to them about how I could stop them from losing business. People who worked *with* Sole Traders such as banking staff or Accountants who looked after small business clients, told me that they would tell their clients about my services. I wasn't trying to attract every kind of business – just the very small, and it worked. Most of my clients still run their businesses from home, with only a few being large enough to take on premises, but they are all small businesses – just like mine, and this is the market I choose to operate in.

TRYING TOO HARD

Another mistake that I've noticed VAs making (but to be fair, many other small business owners have done it too) is along a similar vein to the impersonal 'corporate' language outlined above. When someone hands you their business card from a business you have never heard of before and the telephone number is preceded by (+44) it just has the opposite effect to the desired one. I suspect that the business owner wants to show their business as being one with international links, one that is larger than it is, or just add a touch of glamour to their card, but unless you are representing an international company such as Barclays Bank, it just seems to make the company look inexperienced and small – unless of course your business does have customers internationally such as a translations company.

If you run an international VA business and have client all over the world, then use the International dialing code on your cards and printed communications. However if your business is based in the UK serving a UK market, then why not do everything you can to seem as 'local' as possible? Clients generally prefer to meet those people with whom they are dealing, or at least feel like they can, so being local is a great selling point. Putting a (+44) onto your business card when there is no real need just makes you seem more distant than the next person whose card just shows their area code and number. It's all to do with perception, and as winning business is hard enough, you don't want to make it any harder!

CREATING DISTANCE

Having a 'PO Box' address is another thing to be aware of. When you are working from your own home you may not feel comfortable in putting your home address onto your cards or website, but having a PO Box is another way of distancing yourself from your clients. Building trust and rapport is essential in taking on new clients and they may feel that if you don't trust them enough to tell them where you live, they may not trust you enough to give you their business. I know that I would much rather do business with someone whose business card displays their address as 'Sunnybank Close' or some other obviously residential street name rather than a faceless 'PO Box'. As 'PO Box' addresses are also associated with postal scams and fake lotteries and other such things you hear about on 'Rogue Trader type TV programmes, why would you want to associate yourself with that?

If it really makes you uncomfortable to publicise your address then at least rent a serviced office address or mail forwarding address. Many city centre firms allow their address to be used as a mailing address for small businesses, so choose one of these. It's certainly less faceless and more local to have your address as 'The Media Centre, 100 City Square' or similar, although you will have to pay for the privilege of a prestigious city centre address, so you have to weigh up what's best for you.

LOOKING CHEAP

As perception is such a huge thing when meeting new people for the first time, it pays to invest in a good quality business card – even when you are starting out. There are many internet providers out there who will give you 'free business cards' in return for them printing their own web address and marketing message on the back, but there is limited choice in the styles you can use and they tend to look 'cheap'. Instead of the business having its own identity, it just looks like everyone else, and there's nothing inspiring about that.

There is one card in particular that has a kind of 'moonlight over the sea' image that has been given to me by life coaches, people selling aloe vera products, will writers, party planners, image consultants and dog sitters! Rather than deciding their own identity they have used a template card and it's a wasted opportunity.

When you hand over your business card you have a chance to make a positive impression and giving out a bog standard 'been seen before' card won't make you memorable. At the start of your venture when you have yet to bring in any work it is understandable that you might want to keep costs low by using free business card suppliers, so if you do this just be aware to 'upgrade' your business cards at the earliest opportunity to ensure you are putting out a quality message about your business.

BEING TOO PUSHY

Another common mistake that VAs and small business owners in general can make is with the frequency of which they communicate to their 'prospects'. There is a fine line between keeping in touch with people and 'over contacting' and anyone who runs a business will tell you that there are not enough hours in the day and they are extremely busy, and this is why you need to ensure that your communications to prospective clients actually 'add value' to them and not just clog up their inbox and bother them.

I used to have one contact who sent me an email every few months asking me to update my address and phone details in their address book. This does nothing to add value to me and just serves to take up my time in dealing with the request. After politely responding to the first 3 requests I started to delete all future ones as they became a little annoying. As and when I do have changes to make I will let my contacts know and don't need to be prompted in the meantime. So if you are tempted to 'over contact' people – be aware of how it may come across from their viewpoint.

On the other hand, I met a man at a networking event several years ago who sent me an email follow up after the event which not only told me more about what he did, but it also contained a list of all the upcoming networking events in my region for the coming month. This proved to be extremely useful information and it was the deciding factor in my decision to remain on his circulation list. With hundreds of emails to sift through a week, I prefer to stay off any email lists which don't 'add value' to me in any way. By being clever about what he put in his email and giving me some added value, he gets to send me his newsletter showing who he has helped that month and the list of networking events that is useful to me. It keeps him in my mind for if I hear of someone who could use his services – a very clever marketing trick!

It's good to communicate regularly with 'prospects' if you can – you do need to find a way to be in front of people regularly to get them to think of you when they need you - but always do this in a way that adds value to the potential client. Remember they will always want to know, "what's in it for me?" when they are evaluating whether to let you email them or not, so if you do produce a newsletter or short email with facts and figures on it, ensure that it adds value to the reader.

COPYING COMPETITORS

Another mistake to avoid is copying exactly what a competitor has done or mimicking another company's identity. Not only is it illegal (if you are stepping on Trade Marks or logos for example) but it does nothing to differentiate you from your competitors – and this is the key to winning business. Not only that, it highlights you as someone with no ideas of their own, and when anyone is buying services from another company you know yourself that given the choice you will naturally choose the company who appears to be the more innovative, or more 'up to speed' to assist you. Wouldn't you prefer the organ grinder rather than the monkey - to quote a popular phrase!

Every single person in the world is different and people create businesses that are different. We all have our own unique opinions, outlooks on life, dreams, family situations, career backgrounds and ways of doing things, so we are all capable of being different. Being individual and setting yourself apart from your competitors – the rest of the 'herd' - is what will differentiate you and make your business more memorable in the eyes of your potential clients.

Unfortunately some businesses will copy what a competitor does rather than come up with their own initiatives and it just demonstrates a lack of creativity. You can build a business that is true to your individual nature by finding a niche and sticking to it and working that niche for new customers. Businesses that reflect the owner's personality emit solidness and congruence and it is these 'hard to define' qualities that customers buy into, whether they realise it or not.

I'm all for not 're-inventing the wheel', so the best way to come up with new ideas for your business without copying a direct competitor is to look at different markets and see what they do. For example, if a service based business in a non–competing area does something that you could adapt – why not borrow the idea!

Look at how estate agents attract business, or telecoms companies, or the local restaurant. If they are using an idea that could work for you (such as a customer loyalty card for repeat customers for example) then give it a go! You have nothing to lose and everything to gain by being different and thinking creatively when talking about the kinds of things you do to attract business.

In the chapter entitled 'How To Make Money And Set Your Hourly Rate', I spoke about my Time Bundle pre-payment system. This idea originally came from another service based business in a non competing field and it's also based upon the mobile phone industries' PAYG (Pay as You Go) system.

It's fine to borrow ideas that come from different businesses and adapt them for yours and doing this still makes you unique as a Virtual Assistant. I have to say however that I don't market the Time Bundles system that my business uses to potential clients as it is not as much about them as other points I could promote. In keeping with the 'what's in it for me?' philosophy, anyone hearing that I charge my time in bundles before they have realised the value of working with me might just say, "so what?" It's an irrelevant fact compared to the fact that I can stop them losing business through missed phone calls. So I don't promote this and just raise it when the client has decided to appoint me to help them.

SLOPPY WRITTEN COMMUNICATION

The final rookie 'VA mistake' of this chapter has been saved until last as it has to be the most off-putting and most heinous 'crime' of a modern day Virtual Assistant. With the amount of technology we have at our fingertips to assist us with our documents and with reference books on our bookshelves, we should not be making simple mistakes but many VAs are. I'm referring to spelling errors in written communication. I have lost count of the amount of times a new VA has written to me to ask for advice and their email has been littered with spelling and grammatical errors. It really irritates me and I know that clients of these VAs will not be impressed with such sloppy written communication. It is different if you are familiar with a person, to email them in 'text speak' or to insert the odd ;-) winking smiley face but when communicating with a person you do not know, it's a good idea to err on the side of caution, be professional and double check your spelling.

I can't stress it enough – please, please re-read any written communications before you send them off. Take a few minutes to scan and check there are no typos, no spelling mistakes and that grammatically what you have written is clear. I don't advise relying on your computer's spell check but at least it will catch the glaring errors – you will still need to use your own judgement too. If I see a spelling error on a business website I turn off immediately – don't you? Therefore don't let this happen to you with your potential custom.

A lot of word processing packages with spell checker software will highlight words as wrong or recommend changes to make the spelling an 'American' spelling. They might change 'organisation' to 'organization' when the first is an example of British spelling and the second is written in an international format. If your audience is international then this is ok, but if your audience is British you need to be aware of the correct spellings because spell checkers tend to favour the American spellings!

Several months ago I was at a networking event at a large firm of Solicitors in Leeds where they were doing a presentation on copyright and other intellectual property rights. They had misspelled the word of a very famous sports brand name on their PowerPoint presentation. At first I thought they had done it on purpose to illustrate a point, but they hadn't. It was a mistake and the people round my table and I agreed that it didn't do the best job of promoting this firm as someone to use if we need legal help!

Even professionals make mistakes but something as simple as a spelling error should not have been allowed to happen, especially when you are putting a piece of work in front of the public for scrutiny. You should always be confident that your work would meet the approval of your most critical client. The next chapter goes into how to stay fresh as a Virtual Assistant and remaining ahead of the game…

Staying Ahead Of The Game

No matter how much you love your business, your clients, the work and the freedom, there will be times when it all seems like an uphill struggle. These times usually coincide with periods when there is no money coming in or you have demands for a lot of it to go out! It may also be tough when you are doing your fifth 12-hour day in a row and have not seen your children whilst they are awake! From time to time it happens, and when it does you just need to get through it as best you can.

I've always found that after times where I'm so stacked up with work and am so tired I cannot see straight, that there will be a week or so that is quieter, and when that happens, enjoy it! Start later and finish earlier without any 'guilt'. Go to the gym during the day and take your children out to the park. Divert your telephone to your answering service and relax. Your clients don't need to know that you are having a well-earned break, no one does. But make time to balance out the difficult weeks you've had. There will always be peaks and troughs, but the business owners I've seen who burn out are the ones who don't seem to know when to stop and have some fun. Some people get stuck in a rut and end up working practically round the clock. If you are falling into this trap, step back and think about why you wanted to be a VA in the first place. I bet it wasn't so you could spend a sunny day working whilst your friends and family are sat in the pub beer garden!

STAY MOTIVATED

To stay motivated when times are tough, it's a good idea to re-visit your goals. If you didn't make goals when you started your business, then do it now. Refocus on what you are ultimately trying to achieve and write it down. Somehow when your dreams get committed to paper it makes them more 'real' and what you want is more likely to happen.

Remember what you were hoping to achieve from your business and be strategic about how to make that happen. Things take time to come to fruition and you may have to take some interim 'baby steps' before getting to the place where you can really move forward. If, deep down, you know that ultimately it will all come good and that this business will be what you envisaged, then stick with it. Ride out the rough parts. If you are not so sure, then perhaps you are not as committed to the dream as you thought you were. Double check with yourself that in your heart of hearts you do actually want what you say you want. This is trickier than it sounds, because sometimes we are following a path that someone else has set. Maybe we are trying to gain a parent's approval or please everyone around us and this has shaped a 'false destiny' for us. When we are on a path to getting what we really want, the thing that truly lights our fire, then we would move heaven and earth to get it and it is then that you know you are on the right track.

IDENTIFY YOUR CORE VALUES

A useful way to check that you want what you say you want is to identify your core values. What are the 5 things that are essential to you? Ultimately these will drive your behaviour, whether you know it or not.

A value is something that you will prioritise over anything else, even subconsciously. Have you ever found it such a struggle to achieve something that you thought you wanted? What stopped you from doing what was necessary to achieve it? If you procrastinated until you ran out of time then did a rush job to get it finished, then I'd guess that you didn't really want the outcome you said you wanted enough. Maybe it clashed with another of your core values.

I used to work in a very well paid, high stress job with great employee perks and lots of status, but in return for my rewards I had to be present in the office for long hours, often brought work home and had to squeeze the rest of my life into the weekend when I was also trying to catch up on my rest. Essentially, I had no life – it was all work. As two of my core values are 'fun' and 'freedom' it became clear to me that this was not the true career path for me. I had no freedom and little fun – it just clashed with who I really was.

Money and status are nice to have but they do not form part of my five core values. Stated in such 'black and white' terms it's easy to see where my true destiny was – away from that environment! I willingly gave up the fancy title, money and security to be self-employed but I've never regretted it. I may not have had as much money as I did before, but I have my health, free time, I get to take my daughter to school, I eat well, sleep well, don't need to buy clothes to 'cheer myself up' (as much) and I spend less on petrol and takeaway food! I'm much happier and feel more like 'myself'.

To help you identify your values circle what 'speaks' to you out of the list below. Then decide from those circled which might be a definite value and which would be of secondary importance to you. You will be able to 'chunk it down' until you reach about 5 things that are your 'absolute essentials' and they describe who you are. You wouldn't be 'you' if one of these values were to be removed.

These are your 'core values'. Once you know them you will be able to match them up against what you are saying you want to see if they really do 'fit', because if they don't you may have unwittingly been sabotaging yourself. If your goals are not based upon your values, you will be pulled away from that goal – like it or not!

Honesty	Freedom	Love
Humour	Truth	Respect
Passion	Fun	Credibility
Equality	Individuality	Gratitude
Commitment	Openness	Justice
Accountability	Consistency	Tolerance
Patience	Character	Choice
Reliability	Understanding	Recognition
Status	Competence	Genuine
Fair Play	Authenticity	Integrity
Independence	Endeavour	Power
Learning	Wisdom	Development
Security	Sensitivity	Energy
Kindness	Serenity	Congruence

This is not an exhaustive list but it should give you the idea. Feel free to add your own words into here that describe what is important to you, then keep revising your list until you arrive at 5 words that you could not change or remove. These will be your core values and will shape your goals. Don't worry about choosing words that you think you would *like* to be – the point of this task is to define who you *are* right now, so don't lie to yourself.

It is an enlightening exercise to have a summary of 'you' on paper. I found that by saying out loud what my core values are I was more able to start really being 'me', instead of trying to be something else. This is incredibly freeing.

KEEP GROWING & EVOLVING

When undertaking any kind of transformation or personal development, you will build momentum and move forward in your life and it is the same with your business. In order to remain 'at the forefront' of your competitors and to carry on enjoying the business you have created, it is essential to keep evolving and growing with your experiences.

The suggestions for preparing and starting your VA business in this book involve a lot of background research but no-one ever said that starting in business is easy. Being self-employed is not a route for everyone. It can be a hard slog, a thankless task, there is the uncertainty of whether you will earn enough to live on from month to month, the constant worry about how to bring new clients on board, always having to be 'out there' with a smile on your face to win new business, even when you are not feeling well or in desperate need of some sleep! All of this is done whilst continuing to satisfy the clients you have, ensuring that your own business paperwork is up to date, planning your future marketing, completing book-keeping, ordering stationery supplies, paying bills, attending networking events and so on.

However, the rewards in terms of freedom that come from working under your own terms make it all worthwhile for some. The ability to take an afternoon off when you choose to go swimming, to pick your kids up from school rather than rely on outside help, the feeling of truly making your own money and being in control of your own destiny are often worth giving up the financial security that an employed job gives.

Ultimately there are no shortcuts to gaining the intelligence necessary to create and run a successful business, but this book aims to provide the map of how to get started. Every business will be different because every business owner is different. Some VAs will be prepared to travel to clients' offices or places of business to complete work, some may have wanted to work from home to stop commuting and won't be prepared to work 'onsite', preferring to remain completely virtual. Some will offer every kind of secretarial service possible, some will focus on one area such as book-keeping. Your business will be different to another VAs business and if you have found your niche you are already ahead of the game by making your offer unique.

The best way to remain fresh and ahead of your competitors who may decide to copy what you are doing, is to keep in touch with your clients. Complete regular customer satisfaction surveys – perhaps every 6 months. Remain open to feedback from clients and prospects – a great new idea to propel your business forward might just pop up when you are receptive to it, and by continually asking for customer opinion, you will reassure them that you care about their business and the service levels you provide. You don't want to lose customers who think they are 'not wanted' when this could be avoided with simple, regular contact.

Another good way to inspire ideas on how to keep your business offer fresh is to hang around in the places where your prospective clients are. If you want to assist travelling businesspeople, then have a coffee in the reception area of a popular hotel in your town and observe the various business meetings that are taking place there. Just sit and quietly watch. Absorb the atmosphere. Is anyone struggling to take notes whilst conducting a meeting? Does the hotel provide business facilities such as a fax machine and wireless broadband for business use? Might they be open to the idea of you setting up base in their business area and offering your support services by the hour to the businesspeople within their hotel? This may be an extra marketing tool for them to attract wealthy corporate guests and you would have an ongoing stream of clients that you don't have to go out too far to find.

If you have followed the suggestions in this book to get your business moving, then your ongoing development will be guided by you and your clients. You will come to know which are your best clients, who value your services, who pay on time, whom you get your most interesting work from and once you know this, you can look for more of the same. This will further develop your expertise in a particular area and reinforce your niche.

At one stage of my business I found that I had more Life Coaches than any other kind of business, so I looked for more of them. The fit was good as they charged their own time by the hour, so when they were with their clients they obviously were not doing their own admin or marketing, or answering their own phone. There was a real synergy between my offer and their needs, so I looked at what magazines and newspapers they read, with a view to appearing in them to attract more coaches.

At another stage in my business I noticed that I was taking on more franchise owners for my telephone answering service, so when I went out to networking events I'd focus on people running franchises and tell them about how I could help. The typical situation they were in was that their 'one man band' business had a much larger business impression to their target customers, as their clients recognised the brand name they operated under because of the core franchise. This meant that it was important for the franchise owner to maintain a professional image of their business to live up to expectations and allowing their incoming calls to be taken by an answer-phone just wouldn't do. It created a sloppy first impression of their company and with 'first time' callers more likely to actually hang up on an answer-phone, they were losing potential business through missed calls.

DON'T WORRY ABOUT COPYCATS - INNOVATE

When you are trailblazing, people will always wonder how you are doing it, what you are doing and how they can copy. I say let them! It goes against our usual instinct to protect what we have made, but ultimately if they are not innovative or creative enough to make their own ideas, they are no real threat. Let's face it - how many of us drink 'own brand' supermarket cola? Most of us go for one of the two industry leaders in that market.

Most clients out there will prefer to go with the organ grinder and not the monkey. The person who makes their own decisions and is 'solid' enough to stand on their own two feet and decide how they will operate in any given market is the one whom clients will respect.

The 'copycat' business will always be looking for the next thing to copy and will be 'touchy' about being found out. They are too busy looking back and looking around to be looking forwards. In order to stay one step ahead of the competition and have a business that people will be drawn to then looking forward is the only way to do it.

This isn't to say I haven't looked to the past before for inspiration. I often comment that the wheel doesn't need re-inventing, it does what it needs to do perfectly as it is, so there's no point wasting time and energy on a re-design. However as we 'fast forward' our business lives in the 21st century with applications getting quicker, more multifunctional, more mobile and more user friendly, I've often thought that some 'basics' of business are being forgotten and its' worth re-visiting the past sometimes to see whether any of these business fundamentals can be resurrected.

LOOKING TO THE FUTURE, LEARNING FROM THE PAST

In the 1950s when offices were dominated by typing pools of ladies carrying out basic data inputting and re-typing the same letters to multiple customers, their accuracy and attention to detail was essential. There were no computer spell checkers or easy ways to correct an error – a typing mistake meant that the whole page had to be inserted and typed again. These ladies couldn't afford to waste time on making mistakes, they had to get it right first time. To capitalise on the nostalgic feelings and attention to detail that the phrase the 'Typing Pool' conveys, early in my business before I was fully certain of what direction to take, I experimented with providing a service where I could ensure fast document turnaround within the day, from either dictated notes or audio files. I called this service "The Typing Pool" at The Dream PA. It was a great shortcut to marketing as the well known phrase was already linked in people's minds to accuracy, fast turnaround and efficiency and it therefore instantly communicated to the potential client what they could expect from this service without too much explanation. It's also a great way of demonstrating how the past can give us inspiration in the future!

Nowadays, we are reliant on our technology and might not put as much conscious effort into reading each word as we type it, because we know that if we make a mistake we can always go back afterwards and correct it then without too much trouble. We are probably more productive than the staff of the 1950s as we are all geared up for speed and when we are putting together a document we can just concentrate on getting our thoughts down on paper and then we can re-structure the work to ensure it all makes sense afterwards. But the problem is that some of us don't even do that.

KEEPING UP TO DATE

When you are running your business and trying to stay ahead of the game, it is advisable to stay up to date with what is happening in the world, because it can inform your future marketing by outlining trends to watch; for example, in working patterns. But the difference between being informed and being 'dragged down' is a very fine line. When looking to stay fresh and excited in your business, it's important to manage your general environment, so that you are positive and remain open and proactive. If you read any daily newspaper, you will find that the majority of the 'news' stories are very negative, with only a token positive news story included.

I don't read a daily newspaper, preferring to get my news information from the news bulletins that are broadcast on breakfast television plus I watch the occasional regional local news programme. The television news always gives the news highlights – things that we need to know such as what the bank interest rates are doing or about trends in working patterns, and whilst I may hear a negative news story, there isn't the time for the presenter to go into too much detail, so I am not sucked in by all the 'doom and gloom'. I picked up my husband's newspaper the other day, which I rarely do, and started flicking through it. The paper was full of horror stories, from people being murdered to children putting puppies on a BBQ. I saw that people were having their homes repossessed and 'plastic surgery gone wrong' articles. It was thoroughly depressing and it reminded me why I choose not to read newspapers in the first place! I'm not suggesting cutting yourself off from the rest of the world, but if you are running a small business it can be hard enough to keep going when things get tough and if you take on board too much negativity from outside sources, it could drain you and hinder your personal development and business growth.

STAY MOTIVATED

A great way to stay upbeat and passionate, brimming with new ideas for your business is to listen to motivational CDs or audio files on your iPod or MP3 player. The 'self help' field has grown exponentially in recent years and it is because people enjoy being uplifted whilst getting practical tips of things they can do to let their lives run more smoothly. Tuning in to positive messages and staying 'open' to new ideas and differing viewpoints serves to enhance your creativity and I think that by hearing more positive messages than negative ones, we are creating a confident environment around us which in turn can only make us more productive in our businesses. By surrounding ourselves with positive people, positive messages and pleasant music rather than 'the doom and gloom news', your mindset will change and you will start to look for the good and because you are looking for it, you will see it!

The Future...

Looking forward to the future – how will the Virtual Assistant role change? You are considering an industry that is experiencing huge growth and development and naturally, things will therefore evolve. In the few short years that I have worked as a VA the perception of the role has changed from a VA being 'a secretary who does the typing from home' to a 'Virtual Office Manager' role where the VA is seen as the keeper and protector of a small business's 'Back Office'. As more and more entrepreneurial Virtual Assistants start up their businesses and bring in new ideas and ways of doing business, the face of the industry will change and grow, making it a very exciting place to be.

TELESEMINARS

Virtual Assistants remain a support function to businesses, but they are very often also experts in their own right. Because of their natural talents and credentials in project management they are skilled at getting things done. When they assist a particular niche market of clients they are the ones that are working 'at the coalface' of support in that industry so they are the ones who get to see trends forming and know immediately what the issues facing that niche currently are. If this is you, you can ensure that you stay ahead of the game with your business as a Virtual Assistant by adding extra value through offering teleseminars to your client base, or use teleseminars as a way to attract new clients. This will not only enhance your credibility as a VA that they can count on and whom is up to speed, but if you charge for participation in the teleseminar it can also be an income producing activity.

Conducting teleseminars is a great way to build client loyalty too. Once you have handled enough clients in your business to know where your best clients come from (the ones who pay the most or whom you enjoy working with the most) you can create a teleseminar on a subject of interest to that audience and this is a great way of starting to 'upsell' your services. If the teleseminars are to your existing clients you will be building trust and loyalty by continually making them aware of issues that could affect them. Or you could use the teleseminar to give away information to a new audience, making it a marketing tool to attract new clients to your business and making more money that way. Doing this starts to move you away from just someone who can do the client work that you are appointed for, and it can also make you more of an 'expert' in your field. This is a great label to have when looking for new clients.

VIDEO & BLOGGING

Other 'new' marketing techniques that are starting to gain momentum that you can use within your business are the use of video (look at the popularity of the You Tube[21] website) and blogging. A lot of large companies have started to use blogging to show a 'human' side to their company and millions of individuals and small businesses blog regularly.

Blogging is a way of interaction with your clients and potential clients that you wouldn't normally have through the 'traditional' channels. On a blog you can post relevant news stories or links to websites that your readers might find interesting and so it becomes a resource for information in itself. Blogs are more informal that company websites, and because of this VAs can use them to build up trust and familiarity in the eyes of their potential clients which will speed up the 'getting to know you' process that is often involved with clients when they are looking for some trusted support.

The next chapter gives you some inspiration from people who have successfully set up their Virtual Assistant business.

Virtual Assistant Case Studies

What is wonderful about the VA industry is that the people within it come to the role through so many different channels. Virtual Assistants have all kinds of backgrounds and skills, and have found an industry that can complement their talents whilst giving them a much sought after 'work life' balance.

It is fascinating to hear the stories of how VAs started out, so this chapter contains case studies from 6 very different Virtual Assistants who have made their businesses a success.

LISA P HOGG, MIPA - CHRISALIS SERVICES
www.chrisalisservices.co.uk

I was born in Scotland and my childhood involved moving around a lot, living across the world from Singapore to Somerset! My father was in the Royal Navy so I became used to meeting new people all the time and creating a life for myself very quickly in whatever town or city I found myself in next. I eventually went to boarding school at Harrogate Ladies College in North Yorkshire to study my O-Levels and A-Levels and after this I studied at the Oxford & County Business School. When I left here, I flew to New York on a one-year Scholarship that I was awarded, to work for the Managing Director of a well-known British Bank on Wall Street. Returning from the USA, I worked in the financial district of London for ten years as a PA and Office Manager to Directors and Chief Executive Officers of various large institutions so I was very used to 'high level' corporate life in a fast paced environment.

In 1999 I wanted to concentrate on being near my family so I moved to York where I also met my husband Chris and we got married in 2002. We had a wonderful little boy, Oliver, in May 2004 so not only was I near to my family but I had created my own family with the move! After a couple of years being a home-maker, I decided that I needed to go back to work; not only for financial reasons but also for self-fulfilment. My husband already has his own property development company and I decided that as I had a fully equipped office at home I could become a VA and work from there. I had the skills which I'd gained over my 16 years experience as a PA and Office Manager and I had my first ready-made client - my husband - although working for him was unpaid!

So 'Chrisalis Services' was born in June 2006 offering secretarial, administration and virtual assistance. My husband's property business was called Chrisalis Homes (Chrisalis being an anagram of our names, Chris and Lisa and not just spelt wrong) so it made sense to call my business Chrisalis Services, continuing the brand name. However instead of having the same red/silver butterfly logo which was becoming well known, I inverted the butterfly to form my own logo in silver/red. This has proved to be a wise choice and I feel as though I have a company with a bold image but it is very much a separate company.

I reluctantly joined WiRE (Women in Rural Enterprise) in November 2006 to start business networking. I say reluctantly because it was a lack of confidence that was holding me back, but I needn't have worried as I met a wonderful bunch of ladies – one of whom introduced me to my first paying client – their husband! The business I supported was based in York but didn't have enough cashflow to employ a full time member of staff, although they needed help, so this client really got me on the road!

It was fantastic to be earning money from my skills and the clients grew through word of mouth from there. I am now the Deputy Network Leader of the York Branch for WiRE as I believe in the network so much, and I'm about to start my own networking group called Dynamic Business Divas!

When I started Chrisalis Services my offer was secretarial, administration and virtual assistance but over the years I have grown my services and expanded the company brand name. I now have the following companies under the Chrisalis Services Group, offering business support, event management, design services and PC/IT support:

- Chrisalis Services
- Chrisalis Designs
- Chrisalis Events
- Chrisalis Technical

My clients are mainly start up companies and individuals, as I can offer them tailor made solutions to projects across the board including secretarial, marketing, copy, print & design both in and out of office hours. It's a great boost to be helping other people to get their own companies off the ground, because support is so important.

I love being a VA as it means I can work with a broad range of clients from individuals to small & medium sized companies. I have a technologically advanced office using up to date computers, software and office equipment providing a valuable, cost effective and professional business and personal office support service so I know that technologically, I am at the top of my field.

The work is varied and I'm learning new things every day. I rarely do a project twice and my clients are loyal and return over and over again. I wouldn't change my career and only wish I had started it earlier when I first moved to York as it would have helped me to make friends and settle in sooner. I think that it was lack of confidence that stopped me and I doubted my ability to own a company. I used to work for large corporate banks and emerging market companies where my colleagues were all high flyers with big salaries. It was almost unheard of to set up on your own, so I had no footsteps to follow, which made it doubly hard.

The advice I would give to anyone who wants to become a VA is to think about it in a logical, as well as practical way. I don't think having a computer, a telephone and a printer are the only pre-requisites of starting a home office or VA business, you also need to be sure it's the right path for you too. I'd suggest that you:

- Review your skills and experience.
- Write a business plan and vision for the future.
- Get heaps of professional advice and talk to an accountant, Business Link or advice centre.
- Brand your image and choose a company name wisely to cover a future expanding business.
- Join networking groups and research the internet for free sites to upload your details.
- Read lots of business books, listen and learn.
- Attend workshops and conferences.
- Interact with other VA's and competitors and work together.
- Offer a unique but first class service to your clients, work hard and you'll be a superb VA.

Being a VA is demanding but highly rewarding and I wish every potential VA the very best of luck in setting up their business.

JACQUELINE BREWSTER - VIRTUAL ASSISTANT ONLINE

www.virtualassistantonline.co.uk

My inspiration for becoming a VA came from being 'on the other side of the fence' – as a hard pressed business owner who needed support but couldn't get it! From 2002 to 2005 I launched and managed a professional cleaning franchise business based in Milton Keynes. Throughout this period my business rapidly grew to a turnover of over £250,000 with 17 full and part-time employees and as the business expanded, so did the administrative burden of contracts, payroll, customer correspondence, invoicing, forecasting, marketing and recruitment material.

Ideally it would have been great to employ someone to take care of the 'back-office' duties but with my own rising employment and business costs I could never quite afford to do this. For me it often meant working late into the evening and at weekends - but I just soldiered on, not realising that there was an alternative.

Things changed in 2005. My husband was head hunted to work for another company which meant re-locating more than 200 miles north and we sold the cleaning business as a going concern and moved to the beautiful county of North Yorkshire. It was a dream to find a wonderful rural village to call home and we decided to get a dog and fulfil another of our long held ambitions. Along came Sam (a mad Springer Spaniel) to join our home and we also wanted to expand our family by having a baby. I needed to find a job but I knew I didn't want to go back to full-time employment as I wanted the flexibility of enjoying long walks with Sam and to concentrate on starting a family.

My time as a business owner had polished my office skills and broadened my knowledge of how to run a successful business. I'd gained certificates in typing and shorthand whilst doing my A Levels at school and had always kept myself up-to-date with the latest Microsoft Word, Excel, PowerPoint, Outlook and Sage accounting packages. All that was left was to find a business concept that allowed me to work from home, work the hours that I wanted, as well as satisfy a lot of other people's needs!

This was when I started to think about what really could have helped me when I was a business owner and I realised just how great it would have been to have had a secretary or office resource to tap into as and when I needed it, without the ongoing commitment of employing someone. If financial constraints had prevented me from employing someone full-time in my business, then there must be hundreds of other small business owners in the same position too. I'd heard about an increasing number of business people using 'Virtual Offices' so after many hours of research I knew that this concept was simply meant for me.

I developed my own 'Virtual Office' and by working as a 'Virtual Assistant' I could help other small businesses owners who found themselves in the same position as I had been. They could use my service as and when they needed to without the complication or stresses of employing someone full or part-time. I could work flexible hours allowing me to still take Sam for long walks and when we did eventually start a family I could still work from home with hours to suit. I certainly had the technical skills and the business acumen, so after a lot of investigation and ground work, I launched the business which I called 'Virtual Assistant Online'.

Two and half years later I now have a successful client base which stretches from an Insurance Broker, Management Training Consultant, Radiologist, Charity and a Financial Advisor to a Blacksmith and Fishing Tackle Retailer! The hours I work are varied and projects include the development of marketing material, mail shots, database development, web content management, business sales analysis, transcription services, internet research and general office admin. I now have a beautiful baby daughter and work my business hours (and dog walking!) around the family's needs.

I have even moved house – again! This time to Northumberland and my business was simply packed up with me and unwrapped at the other end! It was fantastic that I was 'virtual' because it meant I didn't need to lose the momentum I'd built up in my business or change my business name or anything like that. I could continue to build upon the business I'd created whilst just re-locating it again. There aren't many businesses where you can just pack up and take all the clients with you!

I have always had an eye on how I can expand, so recently I joined forces with an agency in India to ensure I can provide a round-the-clock service that truly meets all my clients' needs. I'm a regular networker on business networking sites like LinkedIn and Plaxo and the Indian VA firm approached me after seeing me on one of these sites as they were looking for a British partner. I have worked with them on a couple of projects and the great thing about using their help is that with them I can offer a 24-7 service for my clients as the Indian team work when I've finished for the day. The time differences work in our favour and my clients get a faster service!

I love being a Virtual Assistant and would recommend it if you are looking for a career where you can use your professional skills but work in a flexible way. My 'Top Tips' for anyone who wants to set up a 'virtual office' service are:

- Make sure you have the right technical skills and office equipment. Competent typing skills are a 'must' as well as the investment in a decent PC (and laptop if funds allow).
- Spend some time with another Virtual Assistant to see if the job really suits your needs. Ask if

they would be willing to act as a 'mentor' and offer to help out if need be.

- Visit all of your local business network groups and join just one or two that are best suited for you.

- Get yourself a 'Virtual Assistant' qualification or join one of the recognised 'Virtual Assistant' organisations. That way you can keep abreast of what's happening in the industry and take advantage of training courses that will keep your skills and general 'know-how' right up to speed.

- Don't take it for granted that you'll make a huge profit or turnover in the first year so be sure to have some residual funds to tie you over. Keep on top of your cashflow, invoice regularly and ensure all your clients sign a contract that protects both your rights.

Being a 'Virtual Assistant' has many advantages but remember, you may be on your own a lot, so do keep a good sense of humour! Smile a lot and the entire world will smile with you!

CHARLOTTE BURFORD -
BURFORD SECRETARIAL
www.burfordsecretarial.com

Before becoming a Virtual Assistant I spent 11 years working as an Administrative Assistant/PA for a variety of corporations in the fields of Insurance, Accountancy, Surveyors and a large London Law Firm where I underwent extra study to become a Legal PA. I took a Legal Secretarial Course and then studied part time to complete my LLB Law Degree all whilst juggling full time work and running a home, but I changed my life's direction in February 2005.

I had just started maternity leave and my son was born only one month later and my thoughts turned to work and what I would do when my maternity leave was over. I could go back to a job I really enjoyed but risk 12-hour days and the prospect of not seeing my son, leave and rely on my husband's salary, work part time or look at working for myself. I had spent years around highflying career women who wanted children but then spent most of their lives at the office and this was not what I wanted so I had to make a decision. I spent some time trying to come up with a solution which gave me a work/life balance, which would allow me to work and earn an income as well as spend valuable time with my son, plus I wanted to use the skills that I had worked so hard to achieve. This was when I finally came across the term Virtual Assistant (VA).

As I read more and more into it, I decided that this was something I could do and would be excellent at. I would be able to work from home and also spend valuable time with my son. I must admit when I first mentioned it to my husband he thought I was mad, however once I had explained it to him properly and showed him that I had researched the idea of becoming a VA he thought the idea was ideal and gave me his full support. I handed in my notice at the end of my maternity leave and in August 2005 Burford Secretarial launched.

Choosing the name for my new venture was oddly really awkward. Suggestions included Charlie's Office Angles, B-Sec and Virtual Assistant Services, in the end I spent time searching for available domain names trying to come up with an idea. Finally my husband and I said, "shall we see if Burford Secretarial is free?" and it was, so hence Burford Secretarial was born.

The next stage was to get a website up and running. Luckily my husband works in IT and so I had a web designer available at no cost to me. After that I went out and purchased all my equipment: new computer, multi-function printer, software etc. so that I could offer potential clients the best possible service. Although some of the items I purchased I have never used! My comb-binding machine is still gathering dust and I bought hand-help tape recorders (mini, micro and standard) so that I could transcribe tapes from analogue into digital format and these have never been touched!

My office was set up and my business name chosen but I had no clients, so I decided to take a part-time job whilst my business was getting established to keep my mind focused. During this time I put my business into as many free listings as I could find – both on the internet and in paper directories. I also joined the Society of Virtual Assistants and from this I have received a lot of help and support from other members. I also had business cards and postcards printed which I handed out to friends, family and other businesses in the local area.

It took a few months but in December 2005 I got my first client, she was a Student Midwife and needed me to format her essays for her to the standard that the college required, it was only a small job but the boost was fantastic. From here the work gradually started to come in, mainly from my entry in the printed directories or my listing on Society of Virtual Assistants website. Once you get the first client your confidence grows and it snowballs from there. My clients now consist of a Midwifery Student, Recording Studio, Councillor, Local Football Team and Nursing Home amongst others. For a while I continued with my part-time job until I left for maternity leave with my second child in May 2007 and it was after my baby was born that I became a VA full time.

I started really building up my client list from January 2008 when I threw myself into full time VA work and with my new start I decided to expand and add 'call answering' as a service to clients. This seemed like a great idea, but I soon became aware of my limits and couldn't answer the phone for clients with two small children making noise in the house, so I partnered up with a call answering service who take my clients' overflow calls if I am not available. When I have a quiet house I take the calls myself, but at least I have the back up of a team who will answer the phone in a professional manner.

From time to time I link up with other VAs whom I help out when they have more work than they can handle or if they wish to take 'annual leave' themselves. Although there is a myth that VAs are highly competitive, and I suppose we are to a point, there is also a great support network out there of other VAs who are there to help you and also need help themselves.

My business is always evolving and I keep my eyes open for ways I can work more effectively with clients. In January 2009 I decided to revamp my business and launch a new website as I would like to create a niche market as an Audio Typist and Presentation Expert. Although I will still be able to offer the whole range of services I do now, my main expertise lies within audio transcription and presentations and this is work I really enjoy too.

My future plans are to learn about Search Engine Optimisation (SEO) and Rankings with the aim to move my business to the top of search pages and to use the on-line world for networking and gaining new business. I have made a start in educating myself in this area but it is such a huge field I'm going one step at a time. I am also on the lookout for Virtual Assistants that I can work with on an Associate basis myself – just two or three people that I can trust to undertake my work when I wish to take holidays, am off sick or just have too much work to do.

On the whole, I am extremely pleased with my decision to become a VA, this has given me the personal satisfaction of having my own career, running my own business and being able to spend valuable time with my children. It does mean that my working hours can be odd and I often work quite late into the evening, but that is a small sacrifice as I know I will be able to spend more time with my family and choose when I want to work.

If anyone wants to become a VA, the best advice I can give you is:

- Make sure you do your research thoroughly, go on forums and read as much information as possible.
- Only buy the hardware/software that you absolutely need – perhaps as you go along, because you may find that you don't need to use it at all!
- If you need your current salary to pay your bills set up as a VA part-time until you have an established client base and are bringing in the income that you wish to achieve.

- Try to become an Associate for an established VA as this way you might be able to bring in some work whilst you get yourself established.
- Have fun although it is hard work it gives great satisfaction.

TERESA PLUMMER - THE ADMIN AGENCY
www.theadminagency.co.uk

I started as a VA in 2003, although I didn't call myself that then! I was a kind of 'freelance secretary', just working with 3 clients – all of whom were business partners in the same business. They didn't want an employee but they needed admin help, so they each paid me equal amounts and I worked for them in their business. Then one day I was telling my husband's accountant about my work and she said that technically I was 'employed' but without the perks such as holiday entitlement etc. This was because I was basically working for just one firm. She advised me to get more customers so that it would be more like I was running a business. I quickly acted upon her suggestion and took her on as my next paying client!

Not long after one of my sons was in hospital and one day whilst I was with him I found a copy of The Times and read it from cover to cover. There was an article

155

inside about VAs and I realised that it was describing me! I had never heard the term before but it was definitely what I was doing so I started calling myself a VA which made it easier to describe to people what I did for a living!

I started networking as a VA and I started to meet quite a few other VAs too. Some of them had proper business names and I decided that I needed a name for my company. I was mainly doing admin and I wanted to have that in the title, so I went online to see if anything containing 'admin' was already being used. I settled on The Admin Agency as my company name, although if I knew then what I know now, I probably wouldn't have put the word 'agency' into my name! I have had to deal with quite a few enquiries along the way from people who think I run a temping or employment agency!

Once I had my business name I got to work on creating a website and getting headed paper and business cards printed. Even though I would choose a different name if I had to do it all again, I didn't want to lose the momentum I'd already built as The Admin Agency so I made a decision not to change the paperwork or company name because keeping it gives me consistency and longevity. My early jobs were purely typing and data inputting but as the business and client base grew I started to offer book-keeping, audio typing and even telephone answering and diary management, thanks to a very sophisticated phone and computer system!

Once I started going to business networking meetings I picked up more clients. I now assist a Barrister, a Plumber, a Business Coach, a group of Financial Advisers, a company that sells roller-blinds and several others on an ongoing basis. My other projects have included typing for Exeter University and doing administration for a member of The Law Society. The type of company I can assist and also their geographical location is almost irrelevant.

The technology I had at the start has changed so much over the years that it would have been impossible to predict how my business would have developed over time. I have 6 clients whom I actively travel to - I am free to do this as I have cover in the office when I am out. These clients are within a radius of about 30 miles and two of them have moved further away since I started working with them but they are happy to cover the extra travelling costs I bill them to retain my services. As a VA you build up really close working relationships sometimes and it's really flattering when a client chooses to keep you on because of the great working relationship when they have a change in circumstances.

I get my clients mainly through networking and referrals. My existing and former clients often refer me which is always encouraging and I carry out work for a number of other Virtual Assistants which keeps a steady stream of business coming in. The other VAs and I pass work amongst ourselves if we are snowed under at particular times and it's great to have that professional quality and timely backup when we need it.

I have grown the business to include one full time and one part time member of staff, so whilst we manage to keep ticking over sometimes generating enough work for us all can be a challenge! When things get a bit slow I tend to increase my networking activity because I have not yet found an effective method of advertising. Being a Virtual Assistant is better explained in person as sometimes people don't fully understand the concept so I can't see advertising being all that effective.

My office where my team and I work is actually a purpose built log cabin in the back garden! It is a Swedish style lodge with room for 5 people, fully equipped with workstations, computers, phones and high quality printers amongst other equipment. I love being able to work from home and to have a proper dedicated workspace so that I have some work/life balance. I have 4 children and a self-employed husband, so I make a point of leaving my work at 'work' and not bringing it into the house.

The future for my business is looking very exciting, as I have just set up a sister company called "This Is Reception". This business does purely the telephone answering and diary management work and I created it because I found that my clients didn't seem to want the whole package of telephone answering plus the admin - it seemed to be one or the other which they expected, so keeping the businesses separate makes them easier to market.

Using my experience, the advice I'd give to any VA is:

- Do what you are really qualified for and focus on this niche.
- If you need equipment don't buy it until you actually can have paid work to use it for because you could end up wasting money.
- Buy the best printer you can afford and cultivate a good relationship with a stationery supplier – you never know when you'll need them to pull out all the stops for you!
- Make sure your back-ups are as foolproof as possible as it can be disastrous to loose a client's work through a computer crashing.
- Make sure that you have a separate area specifically for work so you can achieve a good work/personal balance.
- Lastly, one of the trickiest things I have found is setting the prices, so get some advice and do your research. I try to keep mine simple both for me and my clients to understand.

LILACH BULLOCK - ASK LILACH LTD
www.asklilach.co.uk and
www.virtualpatraining.co.uk

Prior to setting up my business I was a training manager for a leading food hygiene and health and safety company plus I spent many years as a PA/Secretary working in London, Australia and Israel. I was getting frustrated with my job and wanted more of a work/life balance. I tried to go part time but my previous company wouldn't allow it and my aim was to start a family, so after my daughter came along I started to think about what else I could do. In the end I decided that being a Virtual Assistant would make the best use of my talents and so in October 2006 whilst I was working part time and looking after a lively 2 year old daughter, I set up my business as a VA.

I was very planned and organised from the start (probably due to my career background!) so I researched business courses and went on a few. I wrote a 'two month' action plan of all the things I needed to do, from choosing the company name, deciding upon the company formation, designing my website and the logo.

I must admit that setting up the business was a huge learning curve for me - I didn't even know what the word 'networking' meant (I thought it was something to do with computers!) so when I first had to go to a networking event and deliver a pitch, the thought of it initially terrified me. But I soon found that it was simply talking to other people about my business and learning about theirs and as I can speak with such passion about my company it terrified me less! Nowadays I love networking and really look forward to it and really everyone is as nervous as you on their first meeting so it's not that scary!

The business officially launched at the end of October 2006 and within 10 days I had secured my first client (who is still with me to this day!) Very quickly I learned how much I enjoyed working in this way and within just 3 months my client base grew to 4 regular business owners. It was at this stage that I decided to hand in my notice at my part time job. It felt like a risk to give up my steady monthly salary but the business was proving so successful very quickly at the time, so I weighed up the decision and I have never looked back!

Once I was a full time VA business started to come in quite quickly and I was getting work in from recommendations/referrals as well as from networking meetings. To cope with the workload, I started outsourcing work to other VAs but after several months of this I decided that I needed to take on staff rather than continuing to outsource work elsewhere. I wanted more control over the output and to grow my business, so I started recruiting for staff who could assist me and my clients whilst I continued to oversee things. This concept has worked well for me although managing staff does bring its own set of problems, so I'd advise anyone considering this route to think it through very carefully.

One of the great things about being a Virtual Assistant is the variety. No two days are the same so we could be providing 'typical' PA services such as diary management or arranging meetings right through to organising events, research work, digital transcription, book-keeping, database management and even marketing! We are often asked what we do and I often reply, "What don't we do" as we have a big enough team to handle any task.

Over the last few years the business has expanded considerably with new clients and my team so I'm currently sourcing local offices to relocate the business to which is very exciting! In 2008 I was a Finalist in the Best Mumpreneur category of the Mother@Work 'Mumpreneur of the Year Award 2008' which involved an award ceremony at Downing Street and it was so nice to have my hard work recognised in this very public way. Another highlight of 2008 was setting up the training arm of my business to provide instruction for Virtual Assistants which I do in both a group and 'one to one' setting.

Since I started I've already noticed changes in the VA industry. When I first went networking a lot of people hadn't even heard of a Virtual Assistant, let alone the benefits of having one whereas now it's more common knowledge that businesses can outsource their work to a trusted professional on a 'pay by the hour' basis. This means that in today's market Virtual Assistants not only need to have exceptional PA/Secretarial skills but they also need a very good business acumen in order to succeed and get clients as they will be seen as professionals in their own right.

If I'm honest I wish I had set up the business years ago. I have finally found something that not only I am good at, but that I love, and I feel incredibly fortunate as I can work around my young daughter.

I now spend most of my time on business development and training which I really enjoy and I have even created a 'shop page' on my website to sell resource products to Virtual Assistants. Nothing gives me greater pleasure than receiving my PayPal alerts to tell me someone has bought one of my products! I have definitely made the right choice by becoming a VA and I am still incredibly passionate about running a business.

My tips for aspiring VAs are:

- Maximise membership offers and deals on offer from small business organisations and networking groups. It certainly pays to shop around and do look into all the benefits offered by different membership organisations before making a decision. The Federation of Small Businesses offers a number of benefits to members from telecom packages and options on VOIP to free banking and legal advice.

- It's also worth signing up to small business newsletters to assess which are most useful for you. A number provide offers, discounts and complimentary tickets to events – all handy when you need to keep a close eye on budget and one website I've found useful is Start Up Community. It's free to join: *www.startupcommunity.co.uk*

- Thinking long-term about your website could save you time and money. I've found through experience, that I could have saved time, money and inconvenience if I had known the value of a content management system for my website. A website presence is essential and it's worth investing money to get a professional looking website. You do, however, need to think carefully about how to keep the website up-to-date so get advice and explore the options within your budget.

- Maintain visibility. Some people shy away from the idea of networking. It may seem daunting but when you really understand what it is and how it works, then you will see how you can make it an effective part of your marketing. Maintaining visibility is key and it's important to remember that networking is a slow burn. You must keep the momentum going and should not expect instant results. It's about linking up with people you feel would be useful contacts – the connections may not pay dividends for many months, or even years, but you are investing in the future of your business. Networking is just as much about how you can link people up with others to help solve problems. The more visible you are, and the more useful you can be as a contact, the more business will flow.

- In addition, there are many more opportunities for online networking these days and this is particularly useful for those people who are not immediately comfortable with attending events or find it difficult to fit them into their schedule on a regular basis. Maintaining a profile online, aside from your website, is essential.

- Focus on the customer. It may sound obvious but if you are going to be successful in business then you must focus on your customer, what they want and how they want it. It's very easy to make assumptions about the services you want to offer but you must be absolutely sure that those are what your potential clients actually want. So, focus on the problems you are trying to solve for clients and potential clients – are you saving them time, money, inconvenience? Are you enabling them to access expert skills and/or flexible support? The chances are that all those will be important but you need to have a clear idea about what is most important to those you are targeting. If you can keep that in mind, and reflect that in your promotional materials and activity, then it will help you realise your business aims much more quickly.

MORAG BRAND - OFFICE DIVA
www.office-diva.co.uk and
www.done-in-a-day.co.uk

I fell into my career as a VA by accident! I did a secretarial course after leaving school as 'something to fall back on' and after being sent to the Head Office of Marks & Spencer PLC on a work placement, I fell in love with the idea of being a Personal Assistant. I did a further work placement at the Daily Telegraph and this just convinced me that this was the career for me! However before I had chance to apply for any jobs upon leaving college, Marks & Spencer wrote to me offering me a role as a Department Secretary at their Head Office, as long as I got my RSA qualifications from the college. I had an anxious wait but when my Distinctions came in, I was relieved to accept the job and went to work in their Press Office as a Team Secretary.

I loved working there but after several years I was beginning to wonder if I'd ever leave, and I had so many other ambitions to fulfil before I settled down, so I resigned and went travelling. I worked my way around the world using my secretarial skills as I went – my best role was as an Executive Secretary to the General Manager of a 5* Hotel in Egypt. Upon returning to the UK I got a job with a firm of Architects.

In my secretarial career I have tended to work within media roles. I became used to supporting large publicity departments within retailers which was a fast moving and pressurised environment and I also worked at newspapers. After the position at the Architect's office, I went to the Mail on Sunday to be a Secretary within a team of 100! In the media you have to play as hard as you work and I quickly became used to being out until midnight then back in the office at 8am to deliver a presentation. I loved working at this company and was promoted several times. My most senior level job was Executive PA to one of the Directors at the newspaper which involved a lot of responsibility including organising the Annual Sales Conference which was attended by more than 100 people and the newspaper's Managing Director. I would have stayed there forever – it really was the best job I'd ever had but in 2001 my husband was offered a job overseas so I packed up and went with him and the next few years involved having two children and being a home-maker.

In 2007, with both children at nursery, I wanted to do something to fill the time and also use the secretarial skills that I'd loved using in my previous roles. I became involved with a charity working with disabled and disadvantaged children and helped them with their admin. Whilst I was there a friend suggested that I look at *www.elance.com* where freelance professionals can look for work, so I went online to see how I could use my secretarial skills, make some money and work around my children. This was how I realised that I could work as a Virtual Assistant and so 'Office Diva' was born!

I was originally going to call my business BVAS which stands for, "Bespoke Virtual Assistance Services" but I just couldn't relate to the name. I figured that if I wasn't passionate about it, then how could I expect my clients to be? I needed a catchy, memorable name that reflected my personality and I think of a 'diva' as someone who is an expert in their field – so 'Office Diva' I became!

My business grew really quickly as my friends and contacts were referring work to me at a really fast rate. I didn't even have chance to get my website finished when I had a full order book of clients and then my existing clients would recommend me to others so I had a continuous stream of work! Because of my background in the media I naturally gravitated toward clients that were in the media, advertising and marketing and I could be doing anything from straightforward business correspondence to more complicated CMS system maintenance or affiliate marketing. Media clientele don't necessarily work 'traditional' office hours, so I am flexible to ensure that I can serve my clients when they need it but that I also get quality time with the kids too. I have a team of sub-contractors who I can call upon for support when I need to so I have got the perfect work/life balance!

It's good business practice to continually develop your offer, so I'm always looking for how I can improve and extend my services. I have teamed up with another VA called Kelly Cairns to form the 'Done in a Day' venture where we do what it says on the tin! Kelly and I met as she also assists one of my clients and we have formed a really strong working partnership. I am also working on eBooks, tutorials and webinars to develop my business further. I love helping business people find out how a good VA can benefit their business and I also enjoy meeting other VAs to offer advice or form support networks. Now I cannot imagine my life as anything else but a VA!

My advice for anyone who wants to become a VA is to do what you know. Just as I have a specialist niche in media and marketing, if you have experience in a particular industry then you will already have a head start if you become a VA for this industry, so look at your talents and play to those.

Summary

I hope that this book has boosted your motivation, given you some pointers of where to get started and some ideas on how you can shape your own VA business. It is not intended to act as a complete guide to business - you will find your own ways of doing things as you progress, but you should be able to get started armed with this information.

Ultimately, being a VA is exciting, new and full of possibilities. This emerging market has yet to become 'mainstream' so people starting their VA business now will be ahead of the game and be innovators in this field. As more individuals set up their own businesses in the UK our pool of potential clients grows. If you are looking outside of your immediate area you could trade internationally, then the world would be your client pool!

The most important thing is to enjoy your business, do a great job for clients and have fun. Don't be afraid to go back and re-visit things in your business along the way, tweaking parts here and there until you have the perfect fit. It's only by chipping away gradually that we end up with a masterpiece. Good luck!

...*One last thing!*

I run Virtual Assistant training courses on a tele-course basis for people who want personal, bespoke VA tuition. The courses run regularly and you can register your interest online for a place. If you are interested in working with me and a small group of like-minded people to learn and develop together, simply visit: *www.thedreampa.co.uk/telecourse.html*

Resources

NOTES

1. 'Home Based Secretaries' – source, A Claytons Secretary: *www.vadirectory.net/about.htm*

2. 'Established business' – source, Business Link: *www.businesslink.gov.uk*

3. 'The Coaching Academy': *www.the-coaching-academy.com*

4. Government's 'Enterprise Strategy' – source BERR; Department for Business, Enterprise & Regulatory Reform: *www.berr.gov.uk/whatwedo/enterprise/enterprisesmes/enterprise-framework/index.html*

5. *www.bbc.co.uk/cbeebies*

6. Internet telephony software: *www.skype.com*

7. Download The Dream PA timesheet at: *www.thedreampa.co.uk/free.html*

8. Virtual Receptionist service: *www.dontlosebusiness.co.uk*

9. Business Link: *www.businesslink.gov.uk*

10. Chamber of Commerce: *www.britishchambers.org.uk*

11. BNI (Business Network International): *www.bni.com*

12. BRX (Business Referral Exchange): *www.brxnet.co.uk*

13. Ecademy: *www.ecademy.com*

14. LinkedIn: *www.linkedin.com*

15. Ryze: *www.ryze.com*

16. Boss to Boss: *www.bosstoboss.com*

17. WiRE – Women in Rural Enterprise: *www.wireuk.org*

18. Alliance of UK Virtual Assistants: *www.allianceofukvirtualassistants.org.uk*

19. IAVA – International Association of Virtual Assistants: *www.iava.org.uk*

20. Twitter: *www.twitter.com*

21. You Tube, the website to 'broadcast yourself': *www.youtube.com/index*

ORGANISATIONS & LINKS

When you are starting up a business it's handy to know where you can turn for advice. This section should help by providing some starting points:

ADVANTAGE BUSINESS ANGELS

If you are looking for funds for your business they can put you in touch with investors.
www.advantagebusinessangels.com

BARCLAYS BANK

Offers a package of business advice, services and support including a magazine and free seminars for small businesses.
www.barclays.co.uk/business/starting-a-business

BRITISH BUSINESS ANGELS ASSOCIATION

The only trade association dedicated to promoting angel investing and supporting early stage investment in the UK. *www.bbaa.org.uk*

BRITISH VENTURE CAPITALIST ASSOCIATION

Representing most major sources of venture capital in the UK. *www.bvca.co.uk*

BUSINESS LINK HELPLINE

All you need to know about starting up and running a business. Tel: 0845 600 9006. *www.businesslink.gov.uk*

BUSINESS PLAN HELP

Help writing a business plan for any kind of business plus cash flow forecasting help and other business strategy templates. *www.businessplanhelp.co.uk*

BUSINESS EYE

Help for businesses in Wales. *www.businesseye.org.uk*

BYTESTART

A small business portal offering help on business start up, structure, insurance, banking, legalities etc. *www.bytestart.co.uk*

EVERYWOMAN

An online source of networking and information for female business owners. *www.everywoman.co.uk*

FEDERATION OF SMALL BUSINESSES

The UK's leading business organisation who lobby the Government on legislation that affects small businesses. *www.fsb.org.uk*

MAKE YOUR MARK

This is the campaign to give people in the UK the confidence, skills and ambition to be enterprising – to have ideas and make them happen. *www.makeyourmark.org.uk*

MOTHER AT WORK

An online 'webzine' resource for working mums. *www.motheratwork.co.uk*

NATIONAL FEDERATION OF ENTERPRISE AGENCIES

Support for start-ups, micro businesses and the self employed. *www.nfea.com*

PRINCE'S TRUST

Help and loans for your business if you are aged 18-30. *www.princes-trust.org.uk*

PROWESS

The UK association of organisations and individuals who support women to start and grow businesses. *www.prowess.org.uk*

SCOTTISH BUSINESSWOMEN

The online community for enterprising Scottish women. *www.scottishbusinesswomen.com*

SHELL-LIVEWIRE

A resource for free information and advice for young people starting a business in the UK. *www.shell-livewire.org*

SMALL BUSINESS

Help for all small businesses including guides and tips. *www.smallbusiness.co.uk*

START-UP BUSINESS HELP

Advice for start-up businesses. *www.startups.co.uk*

SUPERMUMMY

A resource for mums who want to create an online business from home. *www.supermummy.com*

THE BAG LADY

A leading online directory and international trading portal of women in business. *www.the-bag-lady.co.uk*

WIRE

The dynamic UK networking and business club for rural women in business. *www.wireuk.org*

WOMEN AT WORK

An online directory of products and services provided by women throughout the UK. *www.womenatwork.co.uk*

About The Author

Nadine Hill is a business mum, entrepreneur and marketing expert, with more than a decade's experience in PR for fashion & lifestyle brands then in the motor industry which makes her contacts book more valuable than her jewellery box!

She created The Dream PA, a boutique virtual assistance business based in Yorkshire serving the world in 2004/05 which focuses on assisting small businesses through telephone answering and admin support. Since then she has started to help other people achieve their dreams of becoming a virtual assistant through her popular short courses.

Passionate about getting things done and managing time effectively, Nadine created 'The Dream PA Busy Book' which is a personal organiser for busy women. Her own Busy Book is groaning under the weight of all the tasks written in there but Nadine enjoys the juggling act of her life that is lived in Yorkshire, UK with her husband, 2 young children and family cat!

Get A FREE 'one month' trial of the essential 'Virtual Receptionist' service for small businesses.

Don't lose business through missed calls. If you are in business, you can't afford to be without it! You may not always be able to answer the phone and your callers may hang up on an answering machine.

Sign up online to have a Receptionist taking your business calls within the hour...

www.dontlosebusiness.co.uk

SECRETS

OF SUCCESSFUL
WOMEN
ENTREPRENEURS

HOW TEN LEADING BUSINESS WOMEN
TURNED A GOOD IDEA INTO A FORTUNE

linda bennett glenda stone geetie singh penny streeter josephine carpenter

michelle mone yvonne thompson helen swaby marilyn orcharton julie meyer

SUE STOCKDALE

www.bookshaker.com

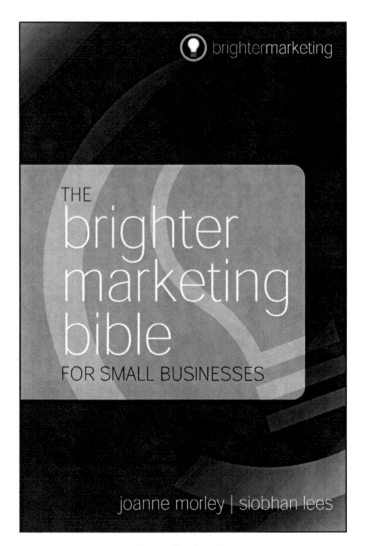

brightermarketing

THE
brighter
marketing
bible
FOR SMALL BUSINESSES

joanne morley | siobhan lees

www.bookshaker.com

www.bookshaker.com